Best Wishes for Christmas
from
Kevin and Kate.
1990.

CONTENTS

APOLOGIES AND ACKNOWLEDGEMENTS

Apologies first of all to my wife, Olwen, who has had to suffer with endless talk of railways and long periods when I have been away from home. Also to my two daughters who have taken in their stride the fact that they have a father with a slightly unusual interest!

Thanks must also be extended to the many people who have helped in all sorts of ways to make this book possible - to those who have accompanied me on visits, and to the railways concerned, which without exception have provided me with the inspiration to see more. Sincere thanks also to the many photographers, too numerous to name individually here, who have made their work available.

Finally, I would like to pay tribute to all those railway employees who have always acted in a helpful manner and done their best to make me feel at home.

Lou Johnson,
Stafford, UK,
June 1989.

THIS EDITION OF 'WORLD STEAM SINCE 1980' HAS BEEN PRODUCED EXCLUSIVELY FOR W.H. SMITH LTD.

Published by Silver Link Publishing Ltd, St Michael's on Wyre, Lancashire, England, PR3 OTG.

Copyright Lou Johnson/Silver Link Publishing Ltd, 1989
ISBN 0 947971 33 5

Designed by Nigel Harris.

Imagesetting by Ps&Qs, Liverpool, Merseyside, England.
Printed in Lisbon, Portugal, by Printer Portuguesa.

FRONT COVER: Steam in Pakistan. An impressive image of working steam in the Indian sub-continent, as 'SGS' class 0-6-0 No. 2470 storms past the photographer whilst working on the steeply-graded branch line linking Khewra and Dandot. As in India, Pakistan's railways were modelled on British practice. *John Laverick.*

TITLE PAGE: Steam in China. On December 12 1984, 'QJ' Class 2-10-2 No. 1792 stands in the yard at Shenyang, awaiting its next turn of duty. The smokebox decorations usually exhort staff to work harder and place safety first. *Gavin Morrison.*

OPPOSITE: Steam in Chile. Although steam in Chile barely survived into the 1980s, dramatic scenes such as this could be seen in many corners of the globe throughout the decade. Indeed, in some parts of the world it is envisaged that the steam locomotive will work on into the 21st century! In China for example, new locomotives were being built until the late 1980s, whilst in Zimbabwe, a refurbishment programme for the country's fleet of Beyer Garratt locomotives was designed to lengthen their lives until at least the end of the 1990s. *Jim Livesey.*

REAR COVER: Steam in the Philippines. The Hawaiian Philippine sugar mill, on the island of Negros, hosted an immaculate fleet of bagasse-fired locomotives. This is Baldwin 0-6-0 No. 5, seen amidst the sugar crop in February 1981. *Tony Eaton.*

INTRODUCTION

I have been lucky enough to sample at first hand most of the railways which operated steam during the 1980s, and it is a privilege to be able to record my experiences and recollections from this period.

This book is by no means a definitive record of steam operation during the period concerned, but more of an introduction to the subject accompanied by some general background information, which I hope will outline the distinctive characteristics which give the railways their individual appeal, unique in each instance. I have not attempted to delve into either locomotive numbers or technical data, as I feel that these subjects are adequately covered in greater detail by other specialist publications. This book is more like a report on a good meal - it tells of the lasting impressions but does not detail the recipes involved!

As you read on you will become increasingly aware of the enormous impact that the steam locomotive has had, even after more than 150 years of continuous operation. From its humble and trouble-strewn

Above: Zimbabwe actually witnessed an increase in steam activity during the 1980s, owing chiefly to a lack of capital for investment in modern motive power. With plentiful coal and a management sympathetic to steam, a large-scale programme of locomotive refurbishment was implemented, which will hopefully ensure that steam will remain operational here until the end of the century. Here, 16A class Beyer-Garratt 2-8-2+2-8-2 No. 614 is seen with a Colleen Bawn-Bulawayo goods, on July 11 1987. *Duncan Cotterill.*

beginnings, it became the power that operated the world's greatest transport system. That the steam locomotive has been superseded by more modern forms of power speaks volumes about its successes. Failures never live long enough to be developed.

My personal fascination with steam power started as a small boy just watching the trains go by from the confines of my push-chair. Yes, I did want to be a locomotive driver and sometimes the idea still appeals. From this predictable start, I was soon to enter the engine-spotting phase, when I spent hours by the lineside, collecting numbers. Eventually, my interest in railways, and steam locomotives in particular, joined forces with a developing desire to see more of the world. This has led me to some out-of-the-way places in the search for steam, visiting corners of the world that see few, if any, foreigners.

Today, I would like to consider myself primarily a railway photographer who wishes to accurately record the atmosphere and environment in which the steam locomotive works. It is the aim of all railway photographers to get that 'once in a lifetime' picture - the elusive 'master shot' – and many of the illustrations supporting the text in this book are superb examples of the railway photographers art. Good pictures, in my opinion, should not be just photographically correct, they must also have that important flavour of being able to capture and evoke the characteristics and atmosphere of the country in which they were taken. Most of the pictures in these pages were taken in the 1980s, but in a number of instances, to illustrate specific locomotives or locations, I have used views taken in the late 1970s. However, this has only been done where the

photograph could still have been taken after January 1 1980. Likewise, there is the occasional view of a special train working, but only where the locomotive and train used were drawn from ordinary service stock.

This book is a tribute to working steam during the 1980s and I feel that it is necessary to define my idea of 'working steam.' Originally, railways were built for the purposes of trade in general and until recent times, always fell into that category. Since the 1960s, many railways have operated steam for museum or tourist reasons and these railways have been omitted from this book. Only those locomotives performing duties over the metals of railways still used for the purpose for which they were originally intended have been included in these pages. This means that although many additional countries used steam during the decade, they have been omitted from this book, as they were employed for museum or recreational purposes.

Lou Johnson,
Stafford, United Kingdom,
June 1989

Above: A quite superb and highly evocative view of Indian steam at sunset at Kharagpur motive power depot as a 'WG' class 2-8-2 and a pair of steam cranes are seen in silhouette against a golden evening sky. *Gavin Morrison.*

Above: In India, steam locomotives provide supplies of both hot and cold water, and also coal, obtained from half-burned firebox ashes. In this picture, village women are collecting hot water from metre gauge 'YG' class 2-8-2 No. 3272 near Donakonda, on the Guntor-Guntakal line, in November 1987.
Peter Lemmey.

Right: In January 1981, Pakistan Railways 'SGS' class 0-6-0 No. 2386 is seen at work in the Khyber Pass, between Jamrud and Landi Kotal. Sister 'SGS' 0-6-0 No. 2511 was at the rear. *John Hunt.*

Above: Scenery and steam at Egridir, in Turkey. On April 11 1985, Class G8 0-8-0 No. 44019 is in charge of the late afternoon departure from Egridir. *Peter Barlow.*

CHAPTER 1:

CHINA

In their early years, the railways of China were linked directly with the commercial and strategic interests of the foreign powers that had gained concessionary control within the nation's boundaries. The system began slowly and it was not until the end of the 1930s that a truly national network had been created. Even then, the total mileage was minute

Facing page: Nancha, in north-eastern China, provides the regular spectacle of trains assisted in the rear by a banking locomotive. On April 5 1988, QJ 286 is assisted by QJ 1987 with a freight bound for the forestry town of Yichun, close to the border with the Soviet Union. *Duncan Cotterill.*

Below: Tangshan Works Erecting Shop, in spring 1987, with a brand new 'SY' class 2-8-2 under the final stages of construction. This works is the last place in the world to regularly build new steam locomotives for the standard gauge. This locomotive can be expected to work until the closing years of the 20th century. *Peter Lockley.*

compared with other countries of similar size and population - the USA for example, where vast systems serving almost every sizeable community had been created, In China, railways were limited to providing links between major cities, and there was little political or commercial interest in developing links with less important areas.

In 1949, when China eventually settled down after the extended hostilities of the Sino-Japanese War, the Second World War and Civil War, the newly-installed Government, led by Chairman Mao, realised that a great step forward had to be made industrially. However, any increase in size of the heavy industrial base could only be achieved with parallel improvements in the nation's infrastructure, especially in transport.

Studies into the problems of transportation were quickly implemented and soon it became apparent that

with the distances involved, the only sound means of transport was the railway. At the time, China was pro-Soviet and the USSR provided large amounts of technical and commercial assistance and soon 'Railway Mania' had reached China. An enormous programme was approved for the construction of new railways, improvement of existing lines and provision of new rolling stock and motive power. Railways were seen to be the sole means for rapid and effective industrialisation and as such were given complete political support, with a very high profile in the internal economy. This provided the base for a similar period of expansion in industry.

By the end of the 1980s, this 'Railway Mania' still had the impetus and strength originally instilled in 1950, with rapid improvements in capacity and capability still making their impact. Today, China has a large network, still incomparable with the USA in route mileage, but with a more positive attitude towards railways. Numerous new routes have been constructed (route mileage has now reached approximately 30,000 miles), many routes have been upgraded from single to double track, and freight and passenger mileages have in-creased considerably. The surprising element of this railway success story is that most of these achievements have been made with steam power as it has only been in recent years that diesel and electric traction have

Above: Double-headed 'QJs' are a common sight on many heavily-graded lines in China. The western part of China, near to Lanzhou, sees frequent heavy traffic amidst excellent scenery. This particular train was photographed at the large horse-shoe curve near to Tianzhu, in November 1987. *Gunter Oczko.*

Facing page, top: QJ 3443, still to be painted, makes its first tentative run during an initial test, in November 1983. The primer paint is probably still wet, for the locomotive is only just off the production line at Datong Works. This scene continued on almost a daily basis throughout the 1980s, with output per year running at roughly one new locomotive per day. An amazing thought in the era of the micro-chip and space shuttle! *Lou Johnson.*

Facing page, lower: Narrow gauge Chinese-style, at Jie-Shi station, on the Langxiang forestry system, in March 1988. This is the daily passenger train which takes all day to make a return journey of around 150km. The passenger stock is based on main line designs, with limited numbers of first class vehicles available, if required. Both locomotives shown here are standard 0-8 0 tender engines which closely follow the outline of their Russian prototypes. *Les Tindall.*

been employed in any significant numbers.

In 1949, China inherited a war-damaged system with a mixed roster of locomotives, originating from many parts of the world. The home-based locomotive manufacturing industry was fairly limited and tended to be influenced by the north-eastern part of the country. With such chaos on the railways China had to rely on

imported engines to assist getting the railway immediately back into operation at the end of hostilities. With increasing Russian influence, efforts were made to expand the construction of new motive power in China and the first post-war examples were based on successful designs inherited by the newly-formed China Railways. By 1958, the first large batches of Chinese-designed locomotives had appeared and with increasing confidence the industry was soon able to provide enough new units for the rapidly expanding system. Main line steam locomotives continued to be built until 1988 when Datong Works finally closed its production lines with 'JS' class 2-8-2s and 'QJ' class 2-10-2s as the last new engines. Although new main line steam power is unlikely to be produced again, the end of decade still saw limited numbers of new steam engines being built for industrial and narrow gauge use.

With large resources of coal, steam was the obvious choice for China Railways, although lack of technical 'know-how' also contributed to the decision. Recent intensive searches for oil have meant that by 1985 a radical change had taken place with diesel and electric traction destined to become ever more important.

Above: QJ 459 rests between turn of duty in the yard at Harbin, on April 3 1988. Although regarded by many overseas enthusiasts as being characteristic of Chinese steam, the smokebox decorations are actually carried by only a few engines. Translation can be difficult, but the phrases usually exhort workers to uphold safety, or to work hard and be efficient! Similar propaganda appears almost everywhere on the railway, from engine shed notice boards to loud-speaker announcements on board the trains. *Duncan Cotterill.*

Although the availability of fuel and skills were two important factors, perhaps the most overriding reason was the effective capital costs of steam. By 1985, a new 'QJ' class 2-10-2 was costing around 150,000 US dollars to construct, compared with 1,500,000 US dollars for new diesel and electric units of comparable capacity. By using steam effectively and efficiently, the Chinese were able to minimise the out-of-service time often associated with this form of power and incredibly high mileages per month were accumulated - equivalent in many instances to what could be achieved with modern forms of traction. With very low labour costs, steam obviously has an edge on commercial viability. For instance, China does not equip its diesel and electric locomotives with a multiple unit capability - the capital cost of the extra equipment is far higher than that incurred by providing extra crews. So, within the Chinese economic parameters, steam still had a large part to play in the development of the nation.

During the 1970s, South Africa and India had provided the steam enthusiast with overseas 'meccas' for steam - but after China opening its doors to foreigners in 1976 it soon became clear that in the 1980s China would take over this role. In 1980, a large percentage of the China Railways network was still featuring complete steam haulage with remaining areas still having plenty of active steam on lesser duties. It was amazing - imagine 3,000-tonne steam-hauled freight trains operating at less than ten minute headways in each direction on a double track main-line - a staggering concept to Europeans – especially when one is reminded that much of the motive power was almost brand new! Locomotive depots provided a similar picture, especially where most of their allocations were for freight duties - a 1985 visit could have seen 1984 and 1985-built 2-10-2s being prepared for their next duty with no old locomotives in sight!

China is a country with wide geographical and climactic differences, from the tropical and often mountainous south, to the chilly plains of Manchuria, where in winter temperatures can stay well below zero for three or four months of the year. Elsewhere in China there are fertile plains, large areas of desert and pleasant, almost European, environments. It was therefore possible to see steam in a variety of settings from steelworks and coal mining areas to tranquil green paddy fields, from snow-laden plains to busy urban areas, and from quiet narrow gauge forestry lines to heavily graded mountain and desert lines. A kaleidoscopic image of steam all within one (albeit enormous!) national boundary.

The first tentative visits to see steam in China were made in the late 1970s, and few embarked on the journey with any idea of what was to be seen. It was a voyage of discovery. On arrival, most visitors were amazed at the volume of traffic and the high level of

Below: The yards to the south of Harbin provided visitors with an-all steam spectacular until diesels appeared in the late 1980s. Steam traction was formerly responsible for all shunting and freight trains departed regularly behind pairs of 'QJ' class 2-10-2s. This view illustrates the quantity of steam that could be seen at many locations in China during the decade - an impressive sight indeed. Nearest the camera is 'QJ' class 2-10-2 No. 854, on December 5 1984. What better sight to inspire the lover of the steam locomotive to visit China? *Gavin Morrison.*

Facing page, top: Baotou Steelworks, in north western China, uses a number of steam locomotives for internal traffic. Here we see a pair of 'YJ' class 2-6-2s at work, in March 1987. Designed solely for industrial use, these lightweight 'Prairies' are based on the larger 'SY' class 'Mikados' and provide their owners with very useful works shunters. *Les Tindall.*

Facing page, lower: The final passenger class to be built in China was the RM 'Pacific', which eventually numbered in excess of 250 examples. One of the class is pictured here in March 1987, departing from Nancha after overnight snow, with a stopping passenger train bound for the regional capital of Jiamusi. The large board above the buffer beam indicates the locomotive's shed allocation - in this case Jiamusi. *Les Tindall.*

Above: A very pleasing rear three-quarter view of 'SL' class 'Pacific' No. 678, standing at Changchun engine shed, awaiting its next turn of duty, on December 8 1984. Always well kept, with boiler bands polished, these engines were to be found on express passenger duties throughout China. They were the first standard 'Pacifics' to be built for China Railways and their design was based on earlier Japanese built locomotives. *Gavin Morrison.*

dependence on the steam locomotive. With more and more of China being opened up to foreigners, visitors were able to explore ever more deeply into the country. There was little variation, however, for it was soon realised that a high degree of standardisation had been achieved on the main-line, where the 'QJs' ruled supreme. Enthusiasts started to look elsewhere, especially at industrial railways, where it was hoped that some older types of locomotives might be found,

and by 1985 most of the major steam centres had been 'discovered', including substantial mileages of narrow gauge networks in the north-eastern forestry areas. By 1989, the 'hidden treasures' had virtually all been uncovered and explored in every detail with, sadly, few surprises.

Since 1950, China has developed the steam locomotive in terms of performance. The 'QJ' class 2-10-2 is an excellent illustration of this point. Originally designed in 1956 as the 'HP' class it went into production in 1958 reclassified 'QJ' ('Qian Jin', literally 'march forward') class. During the 30 years that it remained in production it was improved by the addition of roller bearings, increased boiler pressure, revised blast pipes and numerous other detail differences. The overall effect of these improvements was to increase power from 1,600 hp to 3,000 hp - almost a 100% gain! By the mid-1980s, further development was authorised and David Wardale, who was responsible for the South African experiments of the late 1970s and early 1980s, moved to Datong Works with a brief to increase efficiency and power output even further. By introducing many of the innovative ideas tried in South Africa, the 'QJ2' class was built, on a prototype basis. Again, sadly, it was a case of improvements being made too late and even with impressive gains in performance, once again the future of steam was not to be extended.

CHAPTER 1: CHINA

Facing page: Quadruple track on the main line from Harbin, south to Changchun, provided a flow of double headed 'QJ'-hauled freights running on well maintained permanent way - a typical Chinese scene. Here, QJ 428 leads QJ 2141 on Wong Gong (pronounced 'Wang Gang') Bank, on December 3 1984. Double-heading was preferred for most assisting duties and 'bankers' were only used for short sections. *Gavin Morrison.*

Above: The industrial 'smog' found at all Chinese cities often provides the photographer with superb opportunities. A 'QJ' is pictured in December 1988 with a heavy freight, fully illustrating steam's important role in Chinese industry. *George Shields.*

The flavour of Chinese steam is best explained with a few anecdotal comments. The 'QJ' 2-10-2's are massive engines, complete with an impressive array of modern features, including central heating in the cabs for operation in the extreme cold of the north-east. In addition, they have a very useful steam heated 'oven' for keeping the crews pre-cooked food warm, mounted just along the footplate from the cab. Operationally, China Railways puts great emphasis on efficiency especially in the use of fuel and although the 'QJ's' are equipped with mechanical stokers, more often than not they are unused because hand firing is much more fuel efficient -again a point against modern technology!

An immediate reaction by many people on hearing that a railway is steam operated is to believe it must be old-fashioned and inefficient - a dangerous and incorrect assumption where China is concerned. Heavy traffic levels over immaculately-laid track, with modern colour light signalling, massive freight yards featuring the latest equipment, and all operated by steam seems incongruous - but effective it is, certainly within a Chinese context. When the first visits were made, one obvious place to look for large quantities of steam was locomotive depots. It was quite a while before it was fully appreciated by visitors that China depends on a stabling point system, with relatively few locomotive depots in the accepted sense of the word. Resources - and especially skilled labour – are in short supply, so they are sensibly concentrated at well-equipped depots. It is a system very similar to that employed for servicing and stabling of diesels in Great Britain and another example of how modern ideas are applied to steam power operation. It proves that it is the operators' basic attitude towards steam which deter-mines how well it works, and that when used within a modern framework, steam traction is able to do the job just as well as more modern forms of power.

Above: Tangshan colliery, devastated in the earthquake of 1976, was rebuilt to provide fuel for China's expanding industry. Here, 'YJ' class 2-6-2 No. 272 shunts coal wagons in the yard of No. 1 shaft, on January 9 1987. Scenes such as this will survive well into the 21st century. *David Cox.*

At the start of the 1980s, steam was playing an important role in handling express passenger traffic. The handsome 'SL' and 'RM' class 'Pacifics' were well-suited to this type of train and made an impressive sight as they wheeled along ten and twelve coach trains on the less undulating routes on the plains. Steam became a victim of its own success and as passenger traffic increased it became evident that train lengths would have to be increased to cater for the increasing demand. This soon meant that train weights outstripped the capacity of the 'Pacifics' and dieselisation was the only answer. As the decade passed, fewer and fewer expresses remained in the hands of steam and, at the time of going to press, it was thought that by 1990 all 'Pacific'-worked trains would have gone. Steam performance was always steady, with an ever-watchful eye on coal economy. Speeds were also restricted by heavy freight traffic and consequently, even with modern power, express trains never run at high speeds or start with high acceleration.

One unusual aspect of steam passenger working in China was the use of 2-10-2 freight locomotives in areas where gradients made the large-wheeled 'Pacifics' less-suited to the duties. At the end of the decade there were still areas where steam-hauled passenger working could be experienced using these massive engines.

The steam locomotive in industry is important in China. Almost all industry is strategically placed in areas close to rail links and most factories have private sidings. Many large enterprises have their own locomotives, for internal shunting. Many coal mines and steelworks are almost cities in their own right and the numbers of locomotives can reach 50 or 60. Local passenger services are often operated over their lines to take staff to and from work. It seems that, as in other parts of the world, steam will remain active in industry far longer than on the main line. Tangshan Works was in 1989 still producing small quantities of 'SY' class 2-8-2s designed primarily for industrial use.

Narrow gauge was thought to have been built on a very limited scale in China - although in many ways it would have provided an ideal transport system in many areas of the country. Pre-1948 built narrow gauge steam is very limited in scale, even if one takes into account the short section of metre gauge near to the Vietnamese border. Since the formation of modern China however, many narrow gauge lines with an industrial theme have been built, especially in the forestry areas of Manchuria. Here, 750mm gauge lines using Russian style 0-8-0 tender locomotives have been built to ferry lumber to the main line. During the 1980s, small numbers of new locomotives were being built for these lines at Harbin and it is likely that this will continue sporadically for a few years to come. One area of the narrow gauge scene that has yet to be explored thoroughly is the 'Peoples' Railways' (lightly-laid local lines, for passenger and freight). Many were known to have been built in the 1960s but very few have been investigated. What they hold in store for the enthusiast will be the subject of future exploration and reporting.

In the 1990s, steam in China will take on a less important role and the authorities envisage its complete demise by the end of the century. The retreat will be logical though, as steam will be retained in its final phase on minor lines near to the coal fields - an approach often ignored in other countries.

So, the 1980s belonged to Chinese steam, the last great exponent of this form of power. During this time it helped transform China from economic neglect to full membership as one of the great industrial powers of the world. It is a job steam had done elsewhere in years past and a job that it will probably never do again - unless there is a great surprise over the horizon.

THE INDIAN SUB-CONTINENT

Above: The 'WP' class 'Pacifics' on the Indian broad gauge system certainly have plenty of appeal. Smoke-blackened Erode shed roundhouse, on the Southern Railway, provides a perfect foil to the flamboyant and colourful spectacle of seven bullet-noses awaiting their next turns of duty. *Gavin Morrison.*

The Railways of the Indian Sub-continent were very much an extension of those of the colonial power - Great Britain. Today, the area consists of Pakistan, India, Bangladesh, Sri Lanka and Burma, each with a related railway heritage linked by history.

Following the colonisation of India and the eventual installation of the British authorities, the construction of railways was given unprecedented priority. The 'iron road' was seen as a means of opening up the wealth of the country, a way of unifying the many different States, – and a strategic tool, so that in times of local uprisings, troops could be speedily moved to the area of unrest. Most importantly, they provided material evidence that Great Britain was in charge – and thus they had a psychological impact on the local population. There were other benefits too. The local population was able to transport its produce far more easily, and the impact on the economy was far-reaching. Today, the level of

commerce of the countries that once comprised British India is a direct result of the railways which provided the initial impetus for their development.

Virtually every detail of the railways was imported from the home country, although one major difference did occur - and that was the gauge. Most parts of India used broad gauge - that is 5ft 6in between rails - although in many areas a cheaper option was taken by using metre gauge. Neither of these gauges were used in Great Britain for main-line railways. In addition, extensive local networks of narrow gauge lines (2ft or 2ft 6in gauge) were built, either where the terrain would have made wider gauges too expensive to construct, or

Facing page: Basin Bridge, in Madras, provides an urban background for 'WP' 4-6-2 No. 7262, in charge of a passenger train, with the extensive marshalling yards and power station giving a rather European 'feel' to the view. *Gavin Morrison.*

Left: The cow enjoys a revered position in India and the beasts are allowed to roam freely and this leads to them being seen in otherwise unexpected places. In this view, two cows graze peacefully at the trackside as a 'WP' class 'Pacific' No. 7032 leaves Nagpur with the 0710 to Bhusaval, on October 27 1986. *Duncan Cotterill*

where local population densities provided a requirement for tramway-style connections to the main line railways.

Occasionally, narrow gauge was used for less commercially viable lines, even in the more hostile areas such as the North West Frontier Province (now in Pakistan) where lines were provided to garrison towns. Narrow gauge was even used for railways with a rather more recreational *raison d'etre* - to the hill stations (high altitude resorts used by the British, to avoid the heat of the plains during the summer). Today, these lines survive, linking Darjeeling, Simla and Matheran with the main lines on the plains below. Ootacamund, the hill station for Madras, was graced with a somewhat grander railway - a metre gauge rack line, using Swiss-built 0-8-2Ts which were still operating throughout the

decade, despite extensive rumours about their being ousted by diesels.

To fully understand the railways of the Indian sub-continent one really needs to visit the countries concerned. They are unlike any other systems in the world and exude so much character that one can almost 'drown' in the sensations at a large railway station! It almost impossible to describe the unique bustle and noise, or the unique smells that emanate from every corner, or the large numbers of people that seem to be travelling, using up every space available on trains - including the roof, battery boxes, locomotive tenders or anything that offers somewhere to stand. To say that these railways are the most colourful in the world is almost an under-statement, for they provide the visitor with a unique experience.

Historically, the area has a long tradition of building its own locomotives, although many were imported from the industrial nations prior to Partition, in 1948, when the various independent countries were formed from British India. Since 1948, the majority of new steam locomotives have been built to the designs of Indian Railways which, in keeping with the national policy of making as much on the home market as possible, has expanded the industry so that it can now cope with demand without the need for imports. This has meant that India has been blessed with a large fleet of modern locomotives. Modernisation in the form of large scale electrification and dieselisation has caused a rapid decrease in the operational steam fleet during the decade. However, modernisation has been carried out thoughtfully, rather than simply for the sake of it, as found elsewhere in the world.

The railways of the sub-continent have at their disposal truly vast numbers of unskilled workers. For example, in 1984, Indian Railways was the world's largest employer with a payroll of 1,600,000! When visiting India, it is easy to conclude that the amount of work expands to employ the number of workers available - certainly when there is a crew of seven on the footplate -especially on the narrow gauge ! Tasks which in developed countries would be undertaken by machines with minimal labour costs are carried out

manually in India.........loading ten tons of coal into a locomotive tender by baskets carried on coal loaders heads ....carving the date into wooden sleepers using a mallet and chisel .... sawing through 90lb rail by hand with a hacksaw .... it is all evidence of a completely different set of economic priorities to those we are accustomed to at home.

To consider the Indian sub-continent as a whole is inadvisable. It is an amalgam of different religions, cultures and geographic and climactic areas. Religion has a strong influence in railway catering, for example. The Hindus are vegetarian, whilst the Moslems are non-vegetarian, but do not eat pork. Consequently, as far as railway catering is concerned, separate restaurants must be provided at stations and on board trains. Occasionally, just to add to the variety, one finds western restaurants which are much the same as those dedicated to the Moslem faith – except that they also serve pork!

One unique system employed by Indian Railways is that there are often trains without on-board catering facilities on which you can order food. The passengers

Below: A British-built classic. This 0-4-0, named *Tweed,* was built by Sharp Stewart of Glasgow in 1873 and is seen here working during the sugar cane season at Saraya Sugar Mill on the Ganges Plain. *Gavin Morrison .*

Above: In the 1980s, India's narrow gauge railways provided as much colour and interest as their larger brothers. Here is a beautiful example of narrow gauge steam power, complete with polished brass dome and immaculately polished green livery. *Gavin Morrison.*

requirements are telegraphed ahead and numerous meals are prepared and placed on trays ready for immediate distribution as soon as the train arrives at the catering station. The food is then served by uniformed butlers. The empty plates, utensils and trays are then off-loaded at a later stop and returned to their home base, ready for the next train. It sounds complicated, and it is, especially with all the dietary limitations resulting from religious considerations. It is complex, but it works in a truly Indian way ....from an initial state of chaos everything gets sorted out and everyone receives their booked meal!

Daily train operation has to contend with many problems not encountered elsewhere in the world. The cow, for example, has a revered position in the eyes of the Hindu and almost everywhere on the railway system one comes face to face with these beasts in all sorts of unexpected situations ...... drinking water inside a locomotive depot, foraging for food on station platforms, resting across the tracks or quietly sleeping underneath a goods wagon. Another major problem is the sheer numbers of people that need to be

transported. This causes severe overcrowding on trains, even in normal circumstances. Roof-riding is a common-place and dangerous mode of travel and most frequently seen in the north. The extremes of climate add further difficulties to operating the trains. Imagine hand firing a hard-working steam locomotive when the temperature is 130 degrees Fahrenheit in the shade! The monsoons, with their periods of very high rainfall cause damage to track and structures - many bridges and barrages have to be built to withstand brief but very high rates of water flow. With so many adverse factors affecting operations, it is surprising that trains operate at all. It is due to the dedication, persistence and inexhaustible patience of the staff that the railways provide such an excellent service.

Locomotives had been built in India from quite an early date but never in such quantities to totally exclude imported power. 1948 was a threshold year, when Partition of India into separate independent states meant the end of the old order. India opted for a policy of self sufficiency and developed its own loco-motive construction industry. Subsequently, it has provided large numbers of effective steam locomotives. Production of new broad gauge engines lasted until 1970, when Chiattaranjan Works' in West Bengal, completed the last 'WG' class 2-8-2. Metre gauge loco-motives continued in production a little longer so it was

Top: Bagnall of Stafford (UK) built this diminutive 2-4-0T in 1935 and during the 1980s it was in use on the Eastern Railway narrow gauge line from Shantipur, to the north of Calcutta. *Gavin Morrison.*

Above: An interesting broad and metre gauge comparison with a broad gauge 'WG' class 2-8-2 dwarfing a metre gauge 'YP' class 'Pacific' at Turichchirappalli (known as 'Trichi' for short!) in Southern India. *Gavin Morrison*

not until February 1972 that the same works saw the last 'YG' class 2-8-2 steam locomotive off for delivery to Indian Railways.

In the early 1980s, with the withdrawal of many older classes of locomotive, steam operation became concentrated on more modern designs, especially in India where the post-1948 standard classes began to monopolise traffic. Prior to partition there had always been a degree of standardisation between the various railway companies. Firstly, the British Engineering Standards Association appointed a sub-committee to prepare standard locomotive designs. These initial ideas were eventually modified and by 1906 evolved into the first Indian standard locomotives - commonly known as the BESA designs. After the end of the First World War, it was decided that more powerful engines were required. These became the IRS (Indian Railway Standard) designs. The idea of producing a limited number of standard designs proved very successful and they were generally adopted by all the companies with few modifications. These pre-1948 locomotives all showed a true British character with many classes having a British 'twin.' After Independence, technical assistance to the sub-continent was offered by a broader base of countries, with the USA a major source of input.

Steam hauled express passenger working lasted well into the 1980s, with many principal expresses being in the hands of the handsome bullet-nosed 'WP' class 'Pacifics.' Travelling through India, one soon noticed the wide variety in liveries of the regional systems.

Express train performance in India should not be compared with European standards. Departure from stations is always very slow and lethargic - there are none of those spirited displays typical of King's Cross or Paddington! Subsequent acceleration and maximum speed was tempered by the need for coal economy, with crews being paid bonuses for using less than the allowed quota for the duty. This always meant that time lost en-route was unlikely to be regained, for this would jeopardise a well-earned bonus. Traffic control on single and double tracks is often poor with the result that much time is lost waiting for slower traffic to be turned into loops. Bearing all this in mind, speeds of up to 70mph were regularly achieved and on a good day even 80mph may have been reached.

Maintenance of locomotives has always been a problem, especially within the limited resources

Above: The 'HPS' class 4-6-0s were the standard express passenger locomotive for Indian Railways and they were handsome machines indeed. This Eastern Railway example has long since been superseded by 'WP' class 'Pacifics' and is here relegated to local passenger duties. It is seen at Lalgola shed, being prepared to work a train to Ranaghat, on the Indian Eastern Railway, in January 1982. *Stephen Crook.*

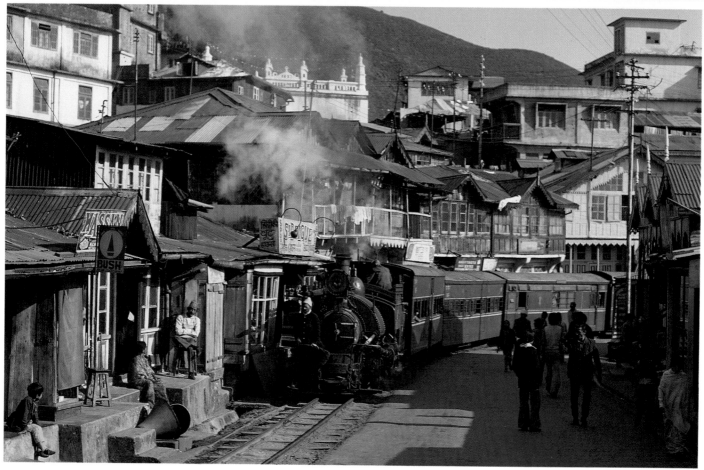

Facing page, top: Besides providing transport power, steam locomotives in India are also a supply of water (both hot and cold) and a meagre source of fuel, for people forage in the depot ashpits for unburned coal. This 'WG' class 2-8-2 has just returned to shed after overhaul and is pictured in ex-works condition. *Gavin Morrison.*

Facing page, lower: The unique appeal of the Darjeeling-Himalaya railway. The town of Kurseong provides passengers with a close look at the local bazaar, for the train runs right outside the traders windows! Here, 0-4-0T No.791, built in 1914, threads its way through the narrow street. *Gavin Morrison.*

Above: Much of the great appeal of the Darjeeling-Himalaya line is its close proximity to the road, which allows photographers to chase the trains by Jeep! The nearness of the road was also a factor in the general decline of the patronage and often one thinks that the only reason why people used the train was that they could avoid paying fares - for fare-dodging (by jumping off the train in this instance!) is almost a national pastime! This train is climbing to Darjeeling, December 1 1984. *Peter Barlow.*

available at most steam depots. Many older engines, and even newer examples nearing their next major overhaul, are relegated to shunting and pilot duties only. Some even suffer the indignity of being branded 'FOR SHUNTING ONLY' in large letters on the cabside, such is their state of disrepair. Lack of resources means that repairs are not carried out proficiently and eventually the locomotive sinks into a very poor state of repair. Finally, the need to keep the locomotive in service calls for drastic surgery. One classic example is the removal of the coupling rods between the front

pairs of driving wheels, usually as a result of excessive sideplay in the axle bearings. The overall effect is that engines originally built as 2-8-2s appear as 4-6-2s and 2-6-4s or even occasionally with different wheel arrangements on each side! Other potentially dangerous temporary measures include the removal of brake blocks and even the wiring down of safety valves!

India is home to one of the most famous railways in the world- The Darjeeling Himalaya line - which uses a fleet of 0-4-0STs, some of which date back to the late 19th century, on its sinuous journey from the broad gauge junction on the plains at New Jalpaiguri to the premier hill resort of Darjeeling, nestling at 8,000 feet above sea level in the lee of some of the world's highest mountains. The journey alone is enough to warrant a visit to India with its breathtaking scenery and diminutive locomotives patiently pulling their trains upgrade into the cool mountain air. Despite many problems during the decade with earthworks being damaged during the monsoons, traffic is still being handled on this spectacular line.

All of India's industry depends on the extensive railway network for bringing in the raw materials and taking out the finished products. To European eyes, much is old fashioned and with limited financial resources available, equipment has to be long-lasting. Thus, the few industrial railways use locomotives which anywhere else in the world would be cherished in a museum or polished on a preserved railway! The

Below: The Himalayas, including Mount Kangchenjunga (8,598m) provide a perfect backdrop in the clear morning air as 0-4-0T No.799 heads the 0700 Darjeeling-New Jalpaiguri train around the famous Batasia Loop. *Hugh Ballantyne.*

Right: In order to gain height rapidly, the engineers were forced to build spirals and tight loops, such as here at the famous Batasia loop. The background scenery provides ample evidence of the topography that the railway encounters on its journey from the Ganges Plain to the hill resort of Darjeeling. One of the ubiquitous 0-4-0Ts (of which up to 20 are active at any one time) heads downhill with a train from Darjeeling to New Jalpaiguri, on December 1 1984. *Peter Barlow.*

WORLD STEAM SINCE 1980

sugar cane mills on the Ganges plain are home to two engines that have passed their 100th birthdays. They were purchased by the mills when their main line service was over and have since had seasonal work at each cane harvest. Such are the delights of steam in India!

Although the railways of the Indian sub-continent all share a common root, 1948 proved to be a watershed year when the countries went their separate ways. Bangladesh and Pakistan were originally united and the railway split into two sections, the East Pakistan Railway (now Bangladesh Railways) and the West Pakistan Railway (now Pakistan Railways). The passing of more than 40 years has caused each railway to acquire its own identity and unique characteristics. With no new steam locomotive designs, as in India, they have continued with the basic roster much as inherited from the colonial past. With fewer classes and less importance given to the railways by the Government, older motive power has lasted far beyond its expected working life. The classic 'SPS' class 4-4-0s (a BESA designed loco) are probably the best example, with many still at work 70 years or more after construction. India had locomotives of the same class at Partition, but with their active policy of new locomotive construction, classes like the 'SPS' were soon withdrawn and replaced by more modern engines. Although Pakistani steam declined throughout the 1980s, increasing problems in keeping the existing

diesel fleet at work meant that the full impact of new diesel orders was never felt. Pakistan thus had pockets where virtually 100% steam operation lasted into the last decade of the century, using an interesting fleet of 4-4-0 and 0-6-0 tender engines. Pakistan has been fortunate that it has never had to cope with the same large numbers of passengers as in India. This has resulted in PR being able to run a railway where service matches demand - which would be an impossible aim in either India or Bangladesh.

Sri Lanka has a compact railway system, reflecting the geographical constraints of the country. Steam locomotives in limited numbers lasted just into the 1980s on broad gauge metals, with a slightly longer life on narrow gauge tracks . The Bangladesh Railway, once part of the East Indian Railway, has suffered from lack of resources, a rapidly increasing population and numerous natural disasters. Steam locomotives in very limited numbers survived into the decade, mostly on shunting duties.

Experiencing steam operations at first-hand can at times be fraught with problems. Obtaining permits to visit steam depots can be a time-consuming and frustrating bureaucratic nightmare. Once obtained, the

Below: India provides some splendid contrasts of scenery, architecture and locomotives. Here, an immaculate 'YP' class 'Pacific' stands at Agra Fort, in November 1982, its modern lines contrasting strongly with the delicate Moghul architecture in the background. *Peter Lemmey* .

permits offer the 'golden key' to an awe-inspiring variety of steam in a cultural environment that is so different to that familiar to us in the more developed world. The steam locomotive crews are amongst the friendliest in the world with their footplate hospitality second to none - footplate tea and curry tiffin are hard to refuse - but do beware of the after-effects!

Railwaymen in every country are resourceful and in India this quality is essential if any sort of operation is to be successful. I remember one night of torrential rain

Top: British-style sema-phore signals galore - many Indian stations seem to have a surplus of signalling, and large gantries are very common. In 1981, a metre gauge 'class 4-6-2 heads out of Jaipur, past two rather modest gantries, as a 'YL' class 2-6-2 arrives with a passenger train.
Gavin Morrison .

Right: Burma Railways' links with Indian Railways were always apparent. Here, a 'YD' class 2-8-2 and a 'YB' class 4-6-2, both also found in India, show their common design features as they await their next turn of duty at Martaban shed, on February 2 1983.
Hugh Ballantyne.

Below: Not all Beyer-Garratt articulated locomotives were large and powerful, as found in South Africa. Here in Nepal, a 2ft 6in gauge example, No.6 *Sitaram*, heads a short train from Khajuri to Jaynagar, just over the border in India. The older Garratts are always distinguishable with their rather severe square tanks - later modified in a more streamlined design. This picture was taken on November 28 1984. *Hugh Ballantyne.*

Left: The number of passengers that a narrow gauge train can carry can be unbelievable! At Khajuri, in Nepal, a couple of tank locomotives, named *Chandra* (right) and *Surjya*, (centre) are seen amidst the general chaos so typical of railway working in many parts of the Indian sub-continent. November 28 1984. *Hugh Ballantyne.*

Below: Pakistan: Landi Kotal at the top of the Khyber Pass branch is the location for an SGS 0-6-0 to do a little over-exuberant shunting. With oil-firing smoke could be be 'made to measure' for the benefit of the photographer! *Gavin Morrison*

Left: The Khyber Pass railway, in the North West Frontier Province of Pakistan, provides a dramatic environment in which the steam locomotive can work. In this view, 'SGS' class 0-6-0s front and rear are providing power for the once-weekly service to Landi Kotal, on the Afghan border. The reversals seen in this view enable the train to gain height rapidly within the limitations of the landscape. *John Hunt.*

before I was due to travel over one of the many narrow gauge lines. On arrival at the station the following morning, with the tracks under six inches of water, I was incredulous when informed by the Stationmaster that the train "had been cancelled due to lack of water." Absolutely astounded at his reply I set about finding the real reason for the cancellation. I discovered that his answer was actually true - the rain had washed away the water tank at the steam depot! However, after a brief discussion, during which I pointed out that I had come a long way to travel on the train, a temporary water pump was erected to fill up the tender from the

Below: Wazirabad shed, in Pakistan, in January 1984, with a brace of 'SPS' class 4-4-0s being prepared for service on the secondary lines that radiate from this location. These locomotives often appeared frail, but were nonetheless capable of pulling eight-coach trains over the almost flat landscape of the area. *Stephen Crook.*

CHAPTER 2: THE INDIAN SUB-CONTINENT

Above: 'SGS' class 0-6-0 No. 2429 departs from Rawalpindi on March 26 1987, with the 1710 to Havelian, a branch line terminus nestling in the foothills of the Himalayas. The westward climb out of Rawalpindi is noted for its severity, but here a 70-years old engine proves that age is no handicap when it comes to hauling a 250-tons load. *Hugh Ballantyne.*

Right: The Pakistan Railway metre gauge system radiates from Mirpur Khas, where it has an end-on connection with the broad gauge system. There are some modern 'YD' class 2-8-2s and a number of classes of older and infinitely more handsome 4-6-0s. On December 29 1987, 'SP' class 4-6-0 No. 140 prepares to leave Naoabad with the 0805 from Nawabshaw Junction to Mirpur Khas. *David Cox.*

puddles; departure was eventually about two hours later than booked!

With more than 40 years since the departure of the British authorities, the sub-continent can be thankful for the one great asset the colonial powers left behind - the railways. Without them their economies would be stifled by the lack of transport. So, steam remains at

work in the Indian sub-continent and will probably still be 'in harness' as the 21st century opens. Steam locomotives -many British-built- have contributed a great deal to the area and even when its job is complete there will be preserved reminders at the excellent railway museum in Delhi .... reminders of one of the greatest steam-worked railways that has ever existed.

Below: Pakistan's HGS class (Heavy Goods, superheated) 2-8-0s displayed all the characteristics of their British roots. Employed originally on heavy goods duties, No. 2216 is seen leaving Kotri Junction with a rather more menial water train, on April 4 1987. *Hugh Ballantyne.*

Left: The narrow gauge system in Pakistan traversed some bleak and uninviting terrain, especially on the Bostan Junction-Fort Sandeman (now Zhob) line. The working conditions for the footplate crew in this sort of landscape can be easily imagined. In this view, a pair of 'GS' class locomotives head an inspection special through the arid country close to Bostan Junction. *Lou Johnson.*

A riverside scene at Malakwal on January 6 1988, as PR 4-4-0 No. 2999 gets under way with a passenger train for Lalamusa. *John Laverick.*

CHAPTER 3

SOUTH EAST ASIA

Railways in this region were influenced very strongly by the colonising powers from Europe, and the differences in character were often surprising. The British, for example, had strong links with their dominions especially in Australia, New Zealand and Malaysia where much was influenced by home-based ideas. The French were the dominant power in South East Asia and bequeathed many examples of their railway prowess which have survived through much strife into the 1980s. An unusual European railway influence could be found in Indonesia, where the Dutch were in power until after the Second World War. It was their only major contribution to colonial railway history and in many aspects was unique. The final colonial influence came in 1936, when the Japanese began to expand their territory. Later, their economic dominance in the area was to have other far-reaching effects on steam and its future.

Below: Indonesian State Railways super-power, as a 2-6-6-0 Mallet No CC5024 struggles along with a train near Cikajang. These locomotives looked very impressive, although in reality years of poor maintenance had significantly eroded their capability. Usually without brakes, the reverser always came in handy for stopping the train! *Peter Barlow.*

Below: The 2-4-0s of the 'B50' class were amongst the most historic engines still at work in the world during the 1980s. Very few modifications had been made to their original design during their working lives and on August 18 1982 No. B5012 is leaving Sleko with the 0500 Slahung-Madiun train, accompanied by the usual motley collection of rolling stock. *Hugh Ballantyne.*

Right: The sugar mill at Soedhono, on the island of Java provides the location for this highly unusual pilot duty! In July 1984, two bullocks are preparing to provide additional power after the steam locomotive had failed to start a heavy load of cane-cars! *J. L. D. Price.*

WORLD STEAM SINCE 1980

Politics have always been connected with railways and the region suffered much from civil war and general unrest during the 1980s. It has meant that much of the steam operation in the region has been inaccessible to the enthusiast, especially in the former French colonies of Vietnam and Cambodia. Here, steam is thought to still have a fairly strong role, but little has been seen to confirm this.

Probably the most fascinating country for steam in the world is Indonesia and more specifically the island of Java. The Indonesian State Railway was operating an incredible variety of locomotive types at the beginning of the 1980s, with some of the oldest and some of the youngest steam locomotives in the world! The Dutch were responsible for building a network of 3ft 6in gauge main lines on the island of Java, supported by a considerable mileage of mostly roadside tramways, similar to their successful counterparts back in the home country. These tramways were lightly constructed and used small engines on light trains.

Above: 0-4-0 tender engines are quite rare, and make fascinating photographic subjects. This Indonesian example is working the Tegal-Prupuk passenger service. The turntable at Prupuk is the location for this tropical scene. *Stephen Crook.*

Left: These powerful 4-6-4 'Baltic' tanks were once used on express passenger services. Relegated to shunting, No. C2813 is seen shunting oil wagons at Purwokerto, on August 16 1982. Visitors remarked that the only freight the railway ever seemed to move was oil wagons, and some would argue that many of these were empty, and moved simply to keep the lines operational! *Hugh Ballantyne.*

Right: No. 52, a 2-6-4T on the north Sumatran system in Indonesia, displays its handsome lines as it shunts at Melangir, in August 1985. Shortly after this picture was taken, the locomotive paused in its duties to enable its bunker to be restocked with timber. *Lou Johnson .*

Below: The Sumatran rack railway system was blessed with some very modern locomotives. Two 'E10' class rack tanks are seen here being prepared for duty at Padang Pandjang in July 1984, prior to working on coal trains. *J. L. D. Price.*

They provided an excellent service to almost all of the island. Elsewhere in Indonesia, railways were limited to three isolated systems on the island of Sumatra and a small system on the island of Madura (off the north-east coast of Java) all built to the Indonesian standard gauge of 3ft 6in. To add interest, many narrow gauge lines, generally 600mm or 750mm gauge, were built to provide internal transportation within the vast and numerous sugar cane plantations on Java and the rather less extensive palm oil estates to be found on Northern Sumatra.

So, at the beginning of the decade, Indonesia was the home to the railway most suited to the title 'working museum'. The roster included such a wide variety of designs and types that often a locomotive depot

containing five or six engines had a similar number of classes! No efforts were made towards standardisation until the early1950s, when a batch of 100 2-8-2s were delivered from Germany.

Interesting oddities included some 2-4-0s built by Sharp Stewart of Glasgow in the1880s, a number of superbly handsome 2-6-6-0 tender and tank Mallets, a small number of 0-4-0 tender engines (which looked as though they were part of some 1930s boxed clockwork train set!) and a seemingly endless array of smaller tank locomotives, including many with full skirting over

Facing page, top: Typical of the many small classes of engine to be found in Indonesia is this Prussian-inspired compound 4-4-0, No. B5132, seen in charge of the morning Labuan-Rankasbitung train, in West Java. *Stephen Crook.*

Above: Steam in North Korea was very much a forbidden fruit for railway enthusiasts until the late 1980s. Pictured here is an example of one of the country's 2-8-2 mixed traffic engines. They bear a marked resemblance to the Chinese 'JF' class from which they are derived. This picture was taken in December 1987. *Les Tindall.*

Right: The Shay is a superb locomotive type, with many moving parts to watch; the gearing and drive shafts are all on the right-hand side of the locomotive. Lopez Sugar Central three-truck Shay No. 10 is seen on February 16 1983, waiting to take a train of loaded cane cars back to the mill on the island of Negros, in the Philippines.

Below: The Hawaiian-Philippine Company engines on Negros have always been known for their immaculate paintwork. On February 15 1983, 0-6-0 No. 7 is propelling empty cane cars into the fields east of the factory. Note the spacious tender, needed for the large quantities of bagasse. *Both: Hugh Ballantyne.*

the motion, acquired from the tramway operations. And that was just on the main-lines on the island of Java !

On Sumatra, the story was no less-complicated. The West Sumatran system had a lengthy section of rack operated main line, taking coal from the mines to the coast at Padang. Here could be found the last additions to the fleet; 17 0-10-0 rack tanks, delivered from Germany and Japan between 1964 and 1967. The North Sumatran system, formerly the Deli Railway, had an operational fleet of 2-4-2, 2-6-4 and 2-8-4 tank engines,

all of obvious Dutch parentage and with the added attraction that they were wood-fired.

Elsewhere, the industrial narrow gauge railways boasted an equally varied fleet of engines. The sugar lines were operating many types of locomotive from 0-4-4-0 Mallet tank engines through to massive and powerful 0-10-0 Luttermollers. These latter engines outwardly appeared to be 2-6-2s, for instead of using connecting rods, the two end axles were geared to their adjacent axles. This gave them the

Left: La Carlota Central sugar mill, in the Philippines, operates a fleet of American-built locomotives. Here an 0-6-0 tender/tank, with an extra wagon for bagasse, prepares for another trip to the cane fields, in February 1981. *Lou Johnson.*

ability to negotiate small radius curves as the side-play on the leading and trailing axles was much greater than with conventional designs. Another interesting type to be found on the sugar lines was a sole example of a rack tank without a rack! The same basic principle of the cylinders driving a lay-shaft was used. The lay-shaft was then geared to the final drive which resulted in a high torque at the wheels for starting heavy trains. It was an interesting idea – but one that could only survive in Indonesia! The Palm Oil Estates on Sumatra had a large fleet of Mallets. They were interesting for the fuel they used - the kernels from the palm oil fruits - which was an economic and practical way of using waste products.

The Indonesian State Railways were reluctant to dispose of anything and even after branch lines had been closed and the track lifted, stations often remained staffed and the daily returns for tickets sales and freight received were still duly completed! The same applied to locomotive depots with no services to work - large ledgers were completed showing the daily mileage each engine had worked even though they had not turned a wheel in months! Long lines of derelict locomotives littered shed yards long after steam had finished in the area. Often, to widespread amazement, a line that had been closed for a few years suddenly re-opened with power provided by one of the ex-derelict engines from the closed shed yard. Such was Indonesia in the 1980s!

The stories of Javan steam are many and varied - some being pure railway farce. The Indonesian State Railway is one of the few systems that uses two forms of coupling and hence requires special wagons with a different coupling at each end! Many have been the times when the train has had the wrong coupling for

the locomotive, and often, to further complicate the issue, the available special wagon has been the wrong way round in the sidings. The complicated shunting manoeuvres resulting from such situations had to be seen to be believed !

The economics of branch line operation in any country are often extremely dubious. In Indonesia, the main reason for their operation was seemingly to increase the salaries of the footplate crews. The service operated by the 'B50' class 2-4-0s from Madiun to Ponorogo was a good case in point. The locomotives were wood-fired and usually the train consisted of a van full of wood (locked in case of theft) together with one or two passenger vehicles ('coaches' being far too good a word for the standards provided). The patronage of the daily train was poor, as a regular bus service running in parallel offered a quicker service throughout the day. En route the crew sold wood from the tender to local villagers who had devised a system of holding aloft a forked stick in which to hold the bank notes at a retrievable height for the crew! The train stayed overnight at Ponorogo before returning the following morning - hence the need to protect the valuable cargo of wood for the following day's sales!

The Philippines, and more particularly the island of Negros, still held an interesting although small fleet of active steam locomotives during the 1980s. With a single exception, they were in use on the sugar plantations where they hauled cane from the fields to the mills. The locomotives were fired by bagasse, the waste vegetable matter from the mill process. However, because of its very low calorific value incredibly huge volumes are needed to produce enough heat to heat the boiler - so much so that enormous tenders were required to carry the fuel, with yet more carried on the

first few wagons of the train. Much of the railway equipment was American in style, although some mills did have a more European influence. Most of the locomotives revealed their US parentage, with impressive arrays of domes ranged along the top of the boiler and very roomy walk-through cabs. Local additions seemed to be numerous, usually fabricated from discarded 40-gallon oil drums - all helping to give a uniquely Philipino flavour to the operation!

The two most notable engines were both Shay-type geared locomotives. The largest was a hefty three-truck Shay at the Lopez Mill, whilst the second was the only locomotive not in use in the sugar industry and was a rather smaller two-truck Shay used at a timber wharf near Hinobaan, on the southern coast of the island. These Shays were to become the last working examples of their breed in daily service; they were once very common on the North American lumber railroads. To see a Shay in operation is a unique experience. Power is transmitted from vertical cylinders mounted in front of the cab to a horizontal shaft which connects to the axles via a series of gears. To hear one approaching on a heavy grade is very strange as the engine seems to be going very fast, owing to the rapid and furious exhaust beat. However, as soon as they come into sight one realises that are perhaps only making ten miles per

hour and it is the low ratio gearing that provides the aural illusion.

Elsewhere in the region, steam reached very low levels of use. Australia could only boast a small amount of steam on industrial lines. Korea had some operational locomotives with the majority in use north of the 39th parallel, although investigation is still required (at the time of going to press) as North Korea may have more steam than originally anticipated. Thailand and Malaysia saw only nominal amounts of steam in service at the beginning of the decade which is a great pity as they both boasted interesting locomotives.

Looking ahead, the area is likely to see nominal steam activity into the1990s, although very little will be in main line use and much will depend on the market value of sugar and the subsequent availability of funds for replacing the remaining rail haulage of cane by road transport.

CHAPTER 4:

THE MIDDLE EAST

Above: Leaving Damascus, Syria, on October 3 1986 is Swiss-built 2-6-0T No. 754, with a short passenger train. The buildings are a mixture of modern blocks and more traditional structures. *Gavin Morrison.*

The railways in this region have not been noted for their steam operation since 1980. The predominant country which used steam traction during the decade was Turkey, with a large network offering a sizeable number of operating classes. Elsewhere, steam has been very limited in use, with many countries only operating steam in emergencies or for visiting groups of enthusiasts.

The middle east has not seen a great deal of railway development, due in part to the low population density and the lack of either industrial or commercial development. Today, the mainstay of the various economies is oil and this is far easier to move in large quantities by pipeline than by rail. Had the oil industry

become more important at an earlier date, then rail development may have been greater. Many railways in the area were built for purely strategic reasons, and as such offered little when the original needs became less important. Many have said that the railways that do still operate would not be missed at all if they all closed - especially outside Turkey.

Another reason for the poor development of railways in the area must be the climate and topography. The

Right: Swiss-built 2-6-0T No. 754, of 1894, heads up the line from Damascus to Beirut with a train for Serghaya. This picture was taken at Tequieh on October 4 1986.
David C. Rodgers.

arid nature of the region is well-known and with large areas of mountainous desert to contend with, construction of railways would always have been difficult. History is always a collection of 'what might have beens' - the British at one time had a strong desire to provide a rail link from Europe to the Empire in India and had this been completed then the story may have been very different. Today, only parts of that dream are in use and with political instability rife in the area, future completion of the link is very unlikely.

Turkey is considered by many to be a European country, but with the majority of its land area east of the Bosphorus, it is truly Asian and follows the religion and cultures of the east rather than those of the west. During the 1980s, most Turkish steam was to be found on its

Asian side with only small pockets of operational locomotives at work on the limited European network. For those who have not visited Turkey, it is basically a high plateau seeing very little rainfall, with a verdant coastal strip. In addition there are some very dramatic mountain ranges of which the Taurus are the most notable.

The construction of railways started with heavy European financial involvement, with Britain providing most of the money. Construction proceeded rapidly and resulted in a system which provided links to all major towns. The TCDD (Turkish State Railway) was established in 1927 and soon acquired most of the independent railway companies. It then set about expanding the network and some 3,000 kilometres of

Above: Turkish 'Skyliner' 2-10-0s always received plenty of attention from enthusiasts. They conveyed the impression of being thoroughly modern machines and were very impressive to see at work. No. 56328, assisted at rear by another member of the class, makes the climb at Alibey amidst scenery typical of Central Turkey. This picture was taken in October 1983. *Gunter Oczko.*

Above: The Izmir suburban service after its surprise return top steam haulage in 1983 - although this was only brief, for on the following day, diesels were in charge once again! Robert Stephenson 2-8-2 No. 46105 leaves Alsancak station, for Buca, whilst a Nohab-built 2-6-0 No. 34060 waits to depart with a Seydikoy service. This picture was taken on August 3 1983. *Stephen Crook.*

WORLD STEAM SINCE 1980

new railway were built. The delivery of new locomotives barely kept pace with the new route construction and with a very pro-German management (certainly as far as steam locomotives were concerned) a predominantly Prussian fleet soon emerged.

During the Second World War, Germany delivered a number of its 'Kriegslok' 2-10-0s, which at the end of hostilities were supplemented by three classes of Allied war engines: the USA standard 'S160' 2-8-0s, the USA 'Middle East' 2-8-2s and 20 British LMS Stanier 2-8-0s. With steam gradually retiring from service during the 1970s, the scene was set for a decade of steam with a predominantly German flavour.

The TCDD embarked on a period of rapid dieselisation during the late 1960s and 1970s - a programme that at times caused more problems than it brought advantages! By 1980, main line working for steam had almost disappeared and was relegated to lengthy sections of secondary mainline, branch lines and the amazing suburban service based at Izmir. In a country well known for its superb scenery, the visiting steam photographer made allowances for the low traffic levels, which were more than compensated by the many heavy grades, dramatic backgrounds and excellent variety of motive power. With some seasonal traffic, mainly sugar beet, double heading was also quite common as the TCDD struggled to move its traffic over the often difficult terrain.

In Britain, the continued use on shunting duties of the faithful Stanier '8F' 2-8-0s caused a high level of interest – but imagine the appeal to the German enthusiast finding engine sheds full of Prussian designs dating back to the First World War: 'G8' class 0-8-0s, 'G10' 0-10-0s and 'G82' 2-8-0s, not seen in Germany for 20 or 30 years !

Turkey was also interesting in its use of fuel. With a

Facing page, upper: The climb out of Izmir was spectacular, with the urban background always adding its distinctive signature to the scene. A TCDD 'Kriegslok' 2-10-0 is seen in August 1983, climbing out of the city on passenger duty, with its cow-catcher painted in typical Turkish style. Stephen Crook.

Facing page, lower: British Stanier Class 8F 2-8-0s amid the mountains at Erzincam shed, in Eastern Turkey. In their home environment, these locomotives always seemed to be quite large; however when seen within the more ample TCDD loading gauge they were dwarfed in comparison with the native loco-motives. The 20 examples sent to Turkey after the war not surprisingly attracted the nickname 'Churchills'. Stephen Crook.

Above: The viaduct at Egridir, on the small system of lines from Burdur, always attracts photographers - and no wonder! Here, 'G8' class No. 44071 climbs away from the station with the afternoon through coach to Istanbul, on August 14 1984. Hans Munch.

large oil industry in the eastern part of the country, oil-fired locomotives were used whilst further west, near the coal mines, coal firing was the norm. When engines were transferred from east to west (or vice versa) the firing system had to be changed along with the tender – a job which made inter-regional transfers quite rare. In practice, this ensured that classes remained largely in their native areas for a number of years.

Although the whole railway had a Germanic 'feel' with motive power, signalling, freight and coaching stock all displaying northern European characteristics, there was one aspect that certainly was not imported from Germany - timekeeping. On one occasion I visited Afyon station during the late afternoon and was surprised to see three steam-hauled passenger trains waiting for departure. They turned out to be the 0500 to Izmir, the 0700 to Izmir and the 0710 to Konya! The two Izmir trains eventually departed at about 1600, one taking the southern route whilst the other took the more direct route through Usak and Manisa. The train to Konya, which incidentally carried a through coach from Istanbul to Kars, left with a flourish at 1700 only to stand at the next loop for two hours whilst some track was replaced by a permanent way gang! The following day this same train was seen entering Konya some 16

hours late! The story did not end here either, as the lonely coach for Van was subsequently seen, more than 48 hours late – some two days later! Moreover, it was still carrying its load of passengers who, apart from normal luggage, had three sheep accompanying them!

One of the most celebrated classes to be found in Turkey were the 'Skyliner' 2-10-0s produced at the Vulcan Ironworks Factory, in the USA. By the way, Turkey was one of the few places in the world where engines from the three different Vulcan Works could be seen in operation: Vulcan Foundry, England, Vulkanof Stettin and Vulcan Ironworks, USA. With a 'skyliner' casing shrouding the boiler top and its fittings, they looked every inch a modern steam engine. Their use was best known over the beautiful line from Irmak, east of Ankara, to the coal mining town of Zonguldak on the Black Sea coast. The route was superb, with heavy gradients commonly providing

Below: It is very difficult indeed to capture the essence of a country in a single photograph - but this excellent picture comes very close to the ideal. This view of a freight train, hauled by a standard 2-10-0, provides a perfect microcosm of Turkey, with the arid mountains topped with snow disturbed only by the sound of the train as its forges upgrade. *John S. Whiteley.*

WORLD STEAM SINCE 1980

Above: Turkey can suffer very badly from the effects of winter, especially in the more mountainous areas. In this view, 2-10-0 No. 56141 is seen near Sozonli on December 30 1985, with the 0532 Erzurum-Kars train. *Ron White/Colourail.*

some of the most dramatic steam spectacles in the country. In contrast, on its final approach to Zonguldak the line skirted the Black Sea, offering superb coastal vistas to passengers.

The area around Burdur became something of a mecca for enthusiasts during September and October each year, when the sugar beet season was at its height. A small network of branches were suddenly transformed from relative tranquillity to a state of hustle and bustle not seen elsewhere in the country. With trains worked mainly by Prussian 0-8-0s and 0-10-0s and double heading very common, it was the ideal place to spend a few days and absorb the atmosphere of a real steam railway doing a worthwhile job. Besides the heavy beet traffic, you could always sample the regular passenger trains, often amounting to no more than one

bogie carriage, which if worked by a 2-10-2, meant that the locomotive was longer than the train ! Pure Turkish delight.

Sadly, by the end of the 1980s, Turkish steam had virtually gone and the chance to sample steam in an Asian atmosphere, yet still comparatively close to home, passed into history. Turkey will be remembered by many as a friendly country where steam provided a service across a large nation, adding in the process another chapter to the incredible history of the area.

CHAPTER 5:

EUROPE

The continent of Europe has had the strongest railway tradition of any part of the World. Even today, after many closures and cutbacks, it has a large network, carrying heavy traffic. In its steam heyday it saw the largest concentration of steam locomotives that the world has ever known. With an advanced economy it became a leader in introducing modern forms of traction, with large scale electrification introduced even as early as the 1930s. After recovery from the Second World War, development gained momentum and by the end of the 1970s Western Europe, apart from a few isolated pockets, was dedicated to diesel and electric traction. In contrast, Eastern Europe developed at a slower rate and even though large scale modernisation had taken place, it was still possible to see large scale steam railway operations, until the late 1970s. The 1980s saw rapid erosion of the remaining steam and by the start of the 1990s only Poland had much to offer the steam enthusiast.

Above: On September 4 1984, a Polish Railways TKt48 class 2-8-2T crosses Lewin Viaduct, in charge of the 1810 Kudowa Zdroj-Klodzko train. Poland was a good example of a country which produced its own engines from the end of the Second World War, and thus added a little extra to the variety of European steam power. *David Cox.*

Each railway in Europe assumed its own national identity. Locomotives were always easily recognisable as being British, French, German or Italian. They took on many of the their national characteristics - British locomotives were always relatively small and handsome, the French machines had style and flair, German engines always had a workmanlike and efficient look, whilst the Italian products displayed a rather eccentric external appearance. Two World Wars did much to blur the national identities and provided the German locomotive industry with enormous influence. The Deutsches Reichsbahn Kreigslokomotiv is a perfect example. Designed for a short life and

Above: The delights of narrow gauge railways in Europe are many and varied. On October 9 1982, East German Saxon-Meyer articulated locomotive No. 99 1561-2 works the Wolkenstein-Johstadt 75cm gauge branch, near Schlossel. *Peter Millar.*

produced in great numbers during the Second World War to provide power for the ever-increasing sphere of German influence in Europe, many locomotives lasted well into the 1980s on a number of European railway systems, including East Germany, Poland and the USSR. In reality, much credit can be given to this one class for extending the life of steam power in Europe. Other standard German classes played a predominant role in main-line and industrial use.

At the end of the Second World War, with a new found optimism, countries which had either existed inside different boundaries, or had not existed before, turned their hand to locomotive design and construction. This added a further strata to the already complicated hierachy. Poland and Czechoslovakia produced locomotives that were new in external design features but which were soon considered as typical steam products of those countries. It is considered by many that Czechoslovakia produced some of the finest looking modern steam engines

during their short years of manufacture (1948-1960) - their large modern tank engines are certainly amongst the finest built in the world.

Railways in Europe had spread rapidly in the 19th century, built mainly as a general means of transportation. The majority were built to standard gauge, although Iberia opted for a broader gauge of 5ft 6in and Russia adopted 5ft 3in, principally to prevent its railways being used as a means of military infiltration by belligerent invading powers. The use of a common gauge did much to assist trade between European countries and the rapid development of the European economy had much to do with railway development..

Many of the railways were economically viable, although with the 'Railway Mania' in full swing, many were rooted more in optimism than realism. Practicality returned eventually and many of the less justifiable routes were built to narrow gauges: 1,000mm, 750mm and 600mm being the most popular. Most of these narrow gauge lines were built to cater for general traffic. However, some were built with much more specific reasons in mind - for example tourist railways. Eventually a large network of narrow gauge lines was constructed with Germanic Europe having the lions share. Some of these lines have survived, especially in the Eastern Bloc, and retained steam operation in the 1980s.

It is often difficult to differentiate between true working steam railways and tourist railways. For tourists, steam is part of the attraction and locomotives may re-introduced from another source. There are, however, a number of routes that were initially built specifically for tourist purposes and have remained that way ever since. In these cases I think that they can be considered as true steam-operated railways, for they are still fulfilling their original purpose. Examples that still use steam power are the Snowdon Mountain Railway in Wales, the Achenseebahn in Austria and the Brienz Rothorn Bahn in Switzerland.

The final working environment for European steam was, yet again, in industry, especially on privately-owned industrial railways. During the 1980s, much surviving steam could be seen in such places: coal mines or steel works were the most common industrial bases for working steam, although forestry railways added a more picturesque aspect to the term industrial.

In Europe, the wheel has almost come full circle, with the virtually complete abolition of steam in normal working service. This has led to the introduction of the museum railway, where steam is operated on a nostalgic basis for the benefit of visitors who wish to relive their past or introduce their transport heritage to their children. I wonder how many visitors to museum railways actually realise how great a part the steam locomotive has played in their history and how much can be credited to its invention ?

Above: Winters in Eastern Europe can be harsh. Snow and frost, while making life difficult for the railwayman, help the photographer considerably in composing attractive pictures. Here, East German 'Pacific' No. 01.0522, leaves Saalfeld, for Leipzig. *Hans Munch.*

Facing page, top: The three-cylinder Class 44 2-10-0s were a masters of their duties. An oil-burning example is seen passing Orlamunde, with a Camburg-Saalfeld freight, in East Germany, in March 1981. *David C. Rodgers.*

Facing page, lower: Transporter wagons provided an easy answer to the trans-shipment problem between gauges. On May 18 1983, Meyer No. 99.1564, on the 75cm gauge line from Oschatz to Mugeln, hauls a freight consisting of standard gauge wagons carried on specially designed 'rollebrucke.' *Graham Lockley .*

WORLD STEAM SINCE 1980

Above: On busier lines, with heavier traffic, the DR uses some powerful 2-10-2 tanks. In this view, No. 99.7247 stands at Ilfeld with the 0942 train from Wernigerode, on April 29 1987. *Graham Scott-Lowe.*

Above: Hungarian Railways depended very much on its high-pitched boiler 4-8-0s of the 424 class, and they became the best-known class operating in Hungary. Equally suited for either freight or passenger operation, they gained an excellent reputation with crews. Illustrated here is No. 424.247, engaged on station pilot duties at Szombathely, on February 1 1985. *Graham Scott-Lowe.*

Left: Working steam engines in Italy survived in very small numbers into the 1980s, with many sheds having only a small allocation. This is a classic Italian locomotive, 2-8-0 No. 740.256, preparing to work a permanent way train at Napoli shed in 1982. *Lou Johnson.*

Above: During the 1980s,The FC Escatron-Andorra line, in Spain, operated this handsome 4-8-4T built by Jung of Germany in 1953, seen here on February 18 1980 with a train of coal 'empties.' *John Toy.*

Above: Spanish Industrial steam has always been full of interest, with some delightful operations. In April 1987, on the metre gauge metals at Sabero, are (on the left) a Sharp Stewart 0-6-0T alongside a much smaller Couillet-built 0-4-0T. *Bob Avery*

Right: The Chiemseebahn, in West Germany has this rather pleasant skirted tram engine which works from Prien to the lake. Typical of many European lines prior to the Second World War, the motion was shrouded so that pedestrians could not become entangled in the working parts. This type of locomotive was exported to many parts of the world and they last saw true service in Indonesia. On August 30 1985, the tram engine is seen leaving Stock, for Prien. *David C. Rodgers.*

Above: The Zillertalbahn, in the Austrian Tyrol, still uses steam traction on a regular basis. A lengthy train is pictured heading along the valley at Strass on August 17 1987, with 0-6-2T No. 3 *Tirol* at its head. The train is the 1540 from Jenbach to Mayrhofen. *David C. Rodgers.*

Right: The Austrian narrow gauge railways were full of charm, and delightful rural scenes such as this did much to increase their popularity amongst enthusiasts. On the Steyer-talbahn, a standard 0-8-2T runs smartly past the camera with a short freight train.
David C Rodgers.

Above: The forestry railways of Romania were a relatively recent discovery for many steam photographers in the late 1980s. In October 1988, 0-8-0T No. 764.421 takes water from a river at Cheia. Note the spark-arresting chimney – essential for steam operations in wooded areas. *Peter Lemmey.*

Although main line steam traction ended in Great Britain in August 1968, in industrial use small locomotives worked on sporadically until the mid-1980s, principally at collieries. At Bedlay Colliery, Glenboig, near Glasgow, this Barclay 0-4-0ST hauled coal to the BR exchange sidings, over a one mile branch line. The locomotive is pictured here at work in April 1980. *Tony Eaton.*

CHAPTER 6:

AFRICA

Above: A stirring sight on June 26 1986, as Class 25NC 4-8-4 No. 3421 leaves Sekonyela siding, with a Bloemfontein-Bethlehem passenger train. The condition of the locomotive is typical of the care and attention still being lavished on these massive machines by their regular crews, even though dieselisation was only months away. The smokebox decorations were a popular embellishment, as were the unofficial nameplates. No. 3421 shared the name *Bethlehem* with other locomotives from this depot. *John Laverick.*

Steam in the 'Dark Continent' during the 1980s witnessed a mixture of decline and rebirth. On the one hand, many countries continued to replace fairly modern steam power with over-technical diesels, whilst at the other extreme, countries like Zimbabwe and Mozambique both introduced major schemes for the rebuilding of existing steam locomotives to extend their working lives.

Africa is the Continent with perhaps the most striking colonial influences. Great Britain, France and Portugal

Below: Kenyan steam only just lasted into the 1980s and here a beautiful example of the British colonial locomotive is depicted: a compact Class 24 4-8-0, No. 2402, is seen shunting at Nairobi. The locomotive is carrying the maroon livery of East African Railways, suitably weathered by the red local soil. *Tony Eaton.*

all exercised a strong influence in railway design and all left their mark on the railways in general and more particularly on steam motive power policy and design.

The first railways on the continent began in South Africa with tentative urban lines offering little to the development of the interior. As technology improved and the need for the opening up of non-coastal areas was given priority by the colonial powers, so the various railways extended their influence to more and more of the continent. As with railways in Europe the

reasons for construction were many and varied with commercial and strategic purposes the most common. However, some railways were built for purely political reasons, with the sole aim of expanding the influence of the resident governing power. The original reasons for constructing lines are long-forgotten today and in many areas it is hard to imagine why a railway was ever built – especially in the more remote and less populated areas.

For most countries, the decade saw a gradual decline

CHAPTER 6: SOUTH AFRICA

Above: Locomotive depots in South Africa always exude plenty of atmosphere - especially at night. In this scene, locomotives wait under the De Aar coaling plant, another typical feature of the SAR, being prepared for their next turn of duty.
John S. Whiteley.

Right: It's July 1982 and South Africa is under nine inches of snow at appropriately-named Withoogte, (White Heights) in the Eastern Cape Province. A '19D' class 4-8-2 is on passenger duty on the Maclear branch, with the 9,30 train from Sterkstroom. Although snow is quite common at higher altitudes, it often remains only for a few hours in the morning, making photography something of a lottery.
David C Rodgers.

WORLD STEAM SINCE 1980

in steam operation – even in South Africa, which during the 1970s was seen as the last major stronghold for steam in Africa. With continuing assistance from the World Bank and other major sources of capital, many diesel locomotives were purchased by the less affluent countries with little regard to their suitability for the rough-and-tumble of daily operation. With a shortage of skilled maintenance and available foreign currency for the purchase of spare parts, the diesels soon became less-efficient in operating terms than the simply-maintained and reliable steam locomotives that they had replaced.

With a greater awareness of this predicament, increased emphasis was placed on suitability of motive power by the late 1980s and as a result there has been a small rebirth of steam, notably in the Sudan, Zimbabwe and Mozambique. With a positive step shown in these areas others may follow the lead, but with a limited number of repairable steam locomotives available, any 'rebirth' will only occur in restricted form. There have been arguments put forward for the construction of new locomotives for Africa, but with governments unwilling to be seen using old-fashioned equipment,

this soundly-based reasoning has largely fallen on rather deaf ears.

One other area which caused considerable optimism amongst railway enthusiasts during the decade was the realisation that steam power had not been developed technically to any significant degree since the 1930s, when available funding for research had been switched to the perceived greater promise shown by modern forms of power. However, since 1980, it has been argued that steam could be re-designed to offer greater efficiency if modern knowledge and technology were applied. Thus, with limited resources a number of experiments were conducted by South African Railways, under the control of David Wardale, in an effort to modernise and improve the capabilities of existing locomotives. This work provided positive and encouraging results, but with a commitment to replace steam power already made by SAR, the initiative was some ten years too late. What is surprising from these experiments (which were conducted with relatively few resources) is that the modified '25NC' 4-8-4 managed to record 4,500 horsepower during trials - quite an achievement on 3ft

Continued on page 68.....

Above: Hopes for an extended life for steam in South Africa were improved greatly with the introduction in May 1982 of the so-called 'Red Devil' modified class 26. The distinctive locomotive is pictured here together with experimental '19D' No. 2644 crossing the Modder River at Perdeberg, during a test run from Kimberley in 1982. *Lou Johnson.*

CHAPTER 6: AFRICA

Above: An imposing view of David Wardale's South African Railways Class 26 No. 3450, known as the 'Red Devil' in tribute to its striking livery. Hopes that this locomotive would help extend the life of main line steam in South Africa came to nothing - the experiments, although successful in improving efficiency, came ten years too late. *Phil Girdlestone.*

Below: A side elevation of the Class 26. *Drawn by Russell Carter.*

Above: 'The Garden Route,' in coastal Cape Province, provides a beautiful setting as Class 24 2-8-4 No. 3627 crosses the lagoon at the final approach to the terminus at Knysna, on the short but scenic branch from George, on September 17 1985. *Duncan Cotterill.*

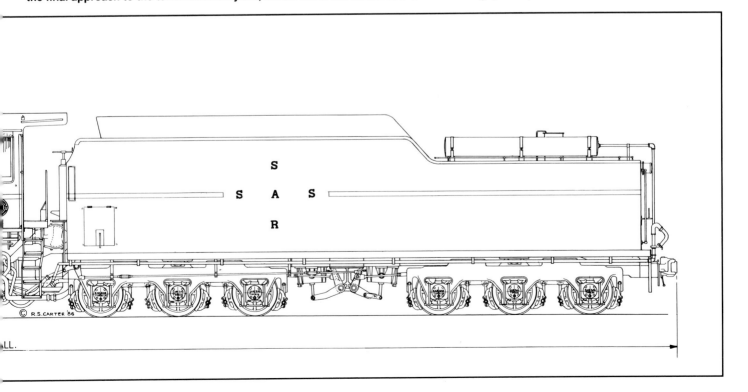

S A R
S A S

© R.S.CARTER '86

LL.

6in gauge, and an indication of what might have been, given different priorities and the political will. Had thought been given to the idea rather earlier, then many locomotives would have continued working much longer than they did.

Zimbabwe, after many years of civil war, had a large steam fleet at the end of the 1970s, assisted by an ageing diesel fleet, all of which had suffered from the ravages of war and poor maintenance. The Railway Authorities decided that steam still had a part to play and a large programme of refurbishment was authorised. The majority of serviceable locomotives were of the Beyer-Garratt articulated design and the best examples were selected for extensive rebuilding. This involved strengthening of the frames, large-scale boiler repairs, new water tanks and coal bunkers, provision of roller bearings and the replacement of many minor components. The success of this scheme has meant that steam still runs in main line use, with the expectation that it will last well into the 1990s. During 1989 the steam fleet was likely to be boosted again with the anticipated purchase of a number of second-hand class 25NC 4-8-4s from neighbouring South Africa to further increase the numbers of available steam locomotives.

Following the National Railway of Zimbabwes' example in refurbishing steam locomotives, US-based aid was made available for a more limited scheme in Mozambique. Thus, a small batch of nine locomotives

Above: For many enthusiasts, the Maclear branch was the epitome of South African branch-line operation. All trains were worked by 19D class 4-8-2s and in this view one of these attractive locomotives is making good progress upgrade at Birds River, with a Sterkstroom-Maclear goods train, shortly after sunrise, in June 1984. *Lou Johnson.*

Facing Page, upper: A classic image of South African steam on the Kaaimans River bridge, in July 1982. Class 24 2-8-4 No. 3627 is working the lunchtime mixed from Knysna to George. *David C. Rodgers.*

Facing Page, lower: The De Aar-Kimberley section of South African Railways will be remembered with much affection as one of the best-known steam-worked railways. In September 1985, a class 25NC 4-8-4 hauls a heavy freight across what appears to be the flat Karoo, but this is deceptive, for the railway climbs a succession of grades, many long and steep, which provide a severe test of stamina for these magnificent engines, and make a taxing call on the skills of the footplate crew. *Duncan Cotterill.*

were dealt with in Zimbabwe on much the same basis as those for NRZ. They will go some way to alleviate the transport crisis in Mozambique and help the country rebuild its war-torn economy without vast amounts of capital being spent on new diesels - money that will be better spent providing food for the inhabitants. Plans were afoot in mid-1989 for a third country to join this growing force - Zambia having considerable numbers of stored locomotives at various sites in the country. Whether this scheme will come to fruition depends largely on forthcoming aid from the West.

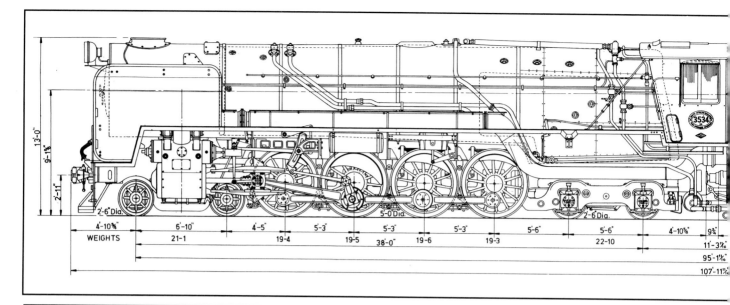

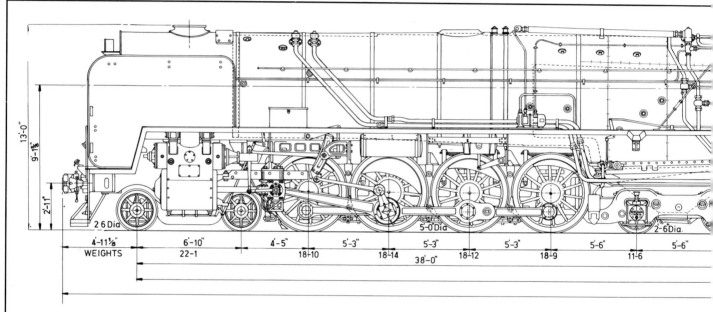

Top & above: Faced with water problems, especially in the Karoo, South African Railways ordered a batch of more than 100 Class 25 4-8-4s, equipped with condensing tenders. Exhaust steam from the cylinders was passed back to the tender where large fans (mounted behind the grilles - top) assisted the condensation process. When the condensing locomotives duties were taken over by diesels, the condensing equipment was removed from both locomotive and tender. A smaller batch of non-condensing locomotives was also built, and known as Class 25NC (above) to which the ex-condensing examples were added. These locomotives employed the best available technology at the time of their design in the early 1950s, including roller bearings and cast-steel bed frames. *Russell Carter.*

Narrow gauge (that is, less than 4ft 8½ in) is considered by many to indicate a railway that is somehow less than real; some people even regard them as 'toys.' However in Africa, metre gauge or 3ft 6in gauge can be considered as 'standard' as they are the most widely-used gauges. Both were used to make construction costs much lower, for earthworks are less expensive and routing is simpler with less restriction on minimum radii of curves than is the case with British standard gauge. It may be argued today that provision of a wider gauge would have produced greater benefits – but it is amazing to see how these narrow gauges have developed into true main trunk line routes. As these pictures show, and as anyone who has visited South Africa will vouch, the locomotives are anything but small!

True narrow gauge (3ft gauge or less) was little-used in Africa, where its main domain was in small feeder

Continued on page 75........

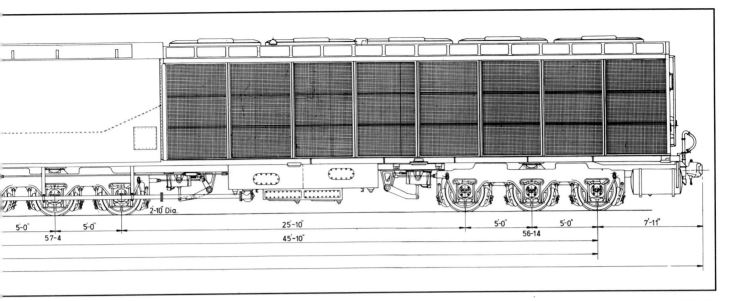

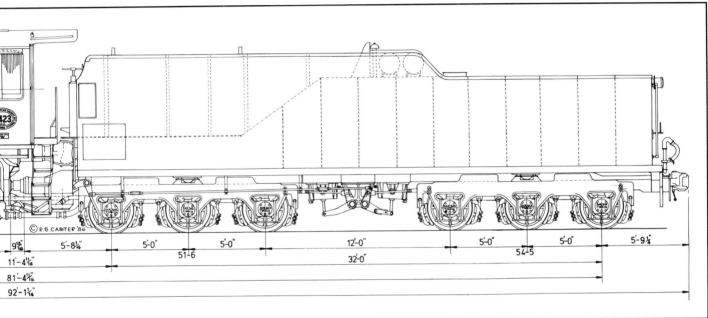

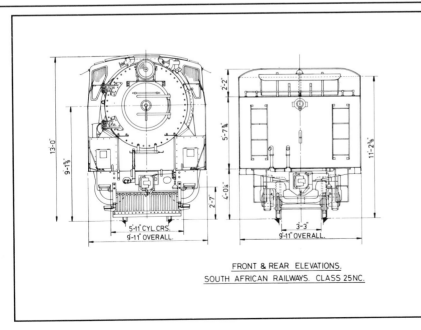

FRONT & REAR ELEVATIONS.
SOUTH AFRICAN RAILWAYS. CLASS 25NC.

Left: Front and rear elevations of the Class 25NC 4-8-4, as rebuilt. The drawings give clear evidence of the massive proportions of these locomotives, with an overall width of nearly 10ft, and running on 3ft 6in gauge track, they operated close to the limits available on this gauge. *Russell Carter.*

Top: A three-quarter official works view of Class 25 4-8-4 No.3536 , as built by the North British Locomotive Company, Glasgow, in 1952. Note the long tender, housing the condensing apparatus, in addition to fuel and water.

Above: Class 25NC (Non-condenser) 4-8-4 No. 3405, in original works condition, and like the upper picture, showing the locomotive in the light grey livery applied for photographic purposes to new locomotives.

Right: A cab view of a brand new Class 25 4-8-4 showing the array of gauges and valves. The large diameter pipe sloping up through the cab floor housed corkscrew-type mecahnical stoker equipment to carry coal from the tender to the firebox. *All: The Mitchell Library, Glasgow.*

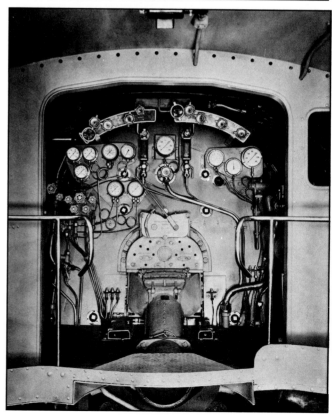

WORLD STEAM SINCE 1980

Class 25NC 4-8-4 No. 3419 approaches Ionia siding on September 21 1985 with the 0830 passenger train from Bloemfontein to Bethlehem. The train is nearing the end of its 12 hour journey worked throughout by the same locomotive and crew, who would stop periodically for water and fire-cleaning. The mechanically-stoked '25NCs' replaced hand-fired locomotives on this duty, which must have been a relief for the firemen, who previously had to shovel about ten tons of coal manually during the journey. *Duncan Cotterill.*

Sunrise - South African style! A 15AR class 4-8-2, built by North British in 1921, storms away from Schoombee with a passenger train bound for Rosmead. Atmospheric photographs such as this really sum up the atmosphere of a working steam railway. *Hugh Ballantyne.*

lines to the main trunk routes. Steam did survive on true narrow gauge lines well into the 1980s, with South Africa having three supreme examples of narrow gauge feeder lines - two serving the timber and sugar cane areas of coastal Natal Province, and the other seeing intensive use during the apple and orange seasons in Cape Province. Elsewhere in Africa, narrow gauge steam only just survived in the war-torn economy of Mozambique with the delightful American-style 750mm gauge line at Joao Belo and the 2ft gauge Sena Sugar Estates system, near the mouth of the Zambesi.

Civil War has been very prominent in Africa during the 1980s, as an aftermath of independence from colonial rule. In 1989, the former Portuguese colony of Angola had yet to settle down to a peaceful existence and very few reports had been made about the level of surviving steam activity. However, it is likely that steam survived in limited quantities to the end of the decade, with the famous Benguela Railway still using its

magnificent wood-fired Beyer-Garratt locomotives.

Africa was a continent for which the Beyer-Garratt locomotive was most suited. Developed in an effort to maximise the power available on lines of light axle-loading, without the need to double head, the Garratt soon became common on most railways of Africa from Algeria in the north to the Cape in the south. It soon became the supreme master of the job, its short, large diameter boiler steaming easily on the long sections of heavily-graded line, with a power output far in excess of what may have been considered normal for conventional locomotives. The British-ruled areas of Africa were especially loyal to the Garratt design especially in East Africa, Rhodesia and South Africa where they formed a sizeable proportion of the operational roster. Their use enabled the increasing of train loadings – with subsequent improvements in potential profitability – over lightly-laid and economically built secondary routes. Many Garratts

Above: Although the SAR closed all the narrow gauge lines in Natal, the section from Port Shepstone to Harding passed into private ownership and now operates as the Alfred County Railway. Seen here in May 1985, prior to privatisation, is an NGG16 class Garratt heading through typically African rural scenery on its northbound journey to Harding, with empty lumber wagons. *Lou Johnson* .

Below: In July 1987, Garratt No. 88 crosses the Umbango River at the head of the 'Banana Express,' the flagship train of the privatised Alfred County Railway from Port Shepstone to Harding. This railway passed into private hands in December 1987, following closure of the 122km branch by SAR on October 31 1986. *Alfred County Railway.*

Right: It's March 31 1988 and the newly-privatised Alfred County Railway's first load of timber comes down from Harding in the charge of Garratt No. 88, seen here leaving Izingolweni. The ACR operates a regular freight service and traffic prospects are said to be good; passenger facilities are also to be upgraded and extended, including the construction of new passenger coaches. The ACR is exclusively steam-worked and the fleet of 2-6-2+2-6-2 Beyer Garratt locomotives are in the care in British steam engineer Phil Girdlestone. His brief as Mechanical engineer at Port Shepstone motive power depot is to improve efficiency and reduce coal consumption, by the introduction of refined exhaust and combustion arrangements. *Alfred County Railway.*

WORLD STEAM SINCE 1980

Above: Combinations of conventional and Garratt locomotives were not especially common in South Africa. In July 1986, a '19D' class 4-8-2 is piloting a GMA class 4-8-2+2-8-4 Beyer Garratt on a freight train from Vryburg to Mafeking, in Northern Cape Province, after a heavy morning frost. *Lou Johnson.*

lasted well into the 1980s and they were in charge of many true main line duties; with their refurbishment in Zimbabwe they look set to continue in service towards the year 2000. Many Garratts were large machines approaching 200 tonnes in working order which on metre or 3ft 6in gauge is undeniably impressive! At the other end of the scale, many Garratts were quite petite in comparison - those on the South African Railways 2ft gauge looked so - but nevertheless still tipped the scales at a deceptive 60 tonnes !

Although Garratts were initially built for lines with heavy grades, they are also able to cope very well with flat, straight sections of road pulling trains at a steady 50mph with ease. A ride on the overnight Bulawayo to Victoria Falls Mail Train proved their versatility beyond doubt. First, they had a train load of about 750 tonnes to haul and over the straight undulating section northwards to Dete, they ran easily at around 50mph. In contrast, north of Thomson Junction, the line twists

and turns as it gains height in the bush with heavy gradients against the locomotive .... and this is where the other side of the Garratt's character shows through. The steady uphill struggle is tackled with gusto, the locomotive frequently blowing off steam from its safety valves – even on gruelling climbing sections of 1 in 40!

The Sudan suffered very badly during the mid-1980s, with drought and subsequent famine. The railway built by the British in their efforts to link the Cape with Cairo had a large but generally unused fleet of neglected steam locomotives which had been discarded as old-fashioned when new diesels arrived. However, in the face of the lack of operational experience, limited capital for spares, and poor maintenance the diesel fleet proved to be as unreliable as the rains. In a practical effort to accelerate the movement of food and supplies to the famine areas, many of the locomotives were given quite minor overhauls so that the railways were able to function in their new role as an emergency food transporter.

The railways of Africa have, during the 20th century, enabled the 'Dark Continent' to become the 'Continent of Hope'. This has been achieved mainly with the help of steam and even today, after many setbacks, steam is still giving its valuable assistance. It has struggled

Early morning and late afternoon provide perfect light for the railway photographer and here a class 25NC 4-8-4 is seen in charge of a passenger train comprised of a varied selection of coaching stock, including some clerestory roofed vehicles. These were produced up to the end of the 1950s, and were still a common sight during the 1980s. *John S. Whiteley.*

Above: The Enyati Railway, in Natal, served one of the most beautifully-located coal mines in the world. Set amongst the hills, the Enyati Colliery was linked by a steeply-graded privately operated branch to the main line at Boomlager, a distance of more than ten miles. Motive power through most of the 1980s was provided by GF class 4-6-2+2-6-4 Garratts, purchased second-hand from SAR. On June 27 1986, No. 2429, in very clean condition, is pictured en route from Boomlaager to Enyati Colliery, with an empty wagon train. *John Laverick.*

through the mountains, across endless deserts, climbed the coastal escarpments and crossed the bush in times of both hope and despair. Even with today's modern transport technology, it is still able to prove its worth as a simply-maintained and very reliable piece of machinery able to do the job for which it was so very well designed. It is also a symbol of what Africa is really all about: this is a continent where modern wonders such as the micro-chip do have their place, but not yet to the same degree as in the more developed countries of Europe and North America. We must learn to limit the introduction of sensitive and delicate high-tech equipment to the areas where it is most effective. The replacement of steam in Africa has been partly recognised as a mistake - rather too late, but at least recognised.

To fully understand the place of steam in Africa during the decade one must first understand the scale in which it operated. In Europe distances between towns are small, distribution of population is dense and the level of commerce and industry is high. In Africa the converse is true - distances between even small

centres of population are high, population density is low and the industrial and commercial centres are spread very thinly indeed. Over half of Africa's railway mileage is in Southern Africa and it is here that industry and the use of natural resources is at its greatest. Elsewhere in the continent, the idea of a railway network is almost unheard of, for there are only a few lines providing limited connections from the coast to the interior. Often, an area rich in natural resources is linked with a coastal port to allow exportation to the world market place.

To be able to stand literally in the middle of nowhere is one of the privileges that Africa has to offer, and to do so near a railway line and hear a hard-working steam locomotive approach, without the noisy distractions of modern urban life, makes one realise the importance of steam in the continent. It is a lifeline to families, factories and commerce. It is often the only outside link to the remote farmer or African villager and even if the train only operates once a week it is of crucial importance to the communities it serves.

I remember talking to the Stationmaster at Jamestown in South Africa, the terminus of a lightly laid branch from Molteno on the East London to Bloemfontein main-line. With a mixed train running on only three days each week he appeared to my European way of thinking to be leading a relatively tranquil existence. However, when questioned it soon became evident that his duties extended far beyond pure railway matters and that his station "was always very busy and there was never a dull moment." Sadly, the line was threatened with closure as this book went to press, but by African standards it was a lot busier than many similar stations in the continent !

Steam operation is not without its unique hazards in Africa. The main line to Victoria Falls passes through part of the Hwange Game Park which is well-stocked with animals of all shapes and sizes. It is not uncommon to see elephant on the line, showing little regard for railways and their operation! More potent a threat to the life of locomotive crews are the big cats, for

Inset: A detail view of the polished cabside numberplate carried by Class 24 No. 3652 at George shed, South Africa, in May 1985. *Brian Dobbs.*

On shed at De Aar in June 1985 are Class 25NC 4-8-4s Nos. 3515 *Judy*, 3473 *Johanna* and 3428 *Selma*. Brian Dobbs

Class 24 2-8-4 No. 3617 skirts the Indian Ocean at Victoria Baai, with the 1255 mixed train from Knysna to George, on September 17 1985. *Duncan Cotterill.*

Above: A Bethlehem to Bloemfontein goods train heads south, away from a water stop, at Fouriesburg, in May 1985. Faced with high ash-content coal, water stops were located at convenient places for fire-cleaning, which were a feature of all SAR steam-hauled services. The interval between fire-cleaning was usually around two hours running.
J.L.D. Price.

Right: South African Railways locomotive cabs were usually kept in beautiful condition - especially where a driver and fireman worked regularly both with each other, and on the same locomotive. This view of Class 25NC No. 3422's cab, at Bethlehem shed, is tribute indeed to the care and attention of its crew. And this is a working locomotive, not a preserved example!
John S. Whiteley

Above: Class 25NC 4-8-4 No. 3417 storms into Sheridan on June 25 1986, with the 3.15pm freight from Bethlehem to Modderport. *John Laverick.*

during the dry season the only source of refreshment can be the isolated water column installed at a remote passing loop in the bush and the animals sense of smell and thirst provides the basis of a potentially dangerous situation.

Steam often lingers in industrial use long after modern power has replaced it in normal railway use. Industry, especially in mining, often has large tonnages to move within its own boundaries. Furthermore, for coal mines especially, what better than to use steam locomotives? But don't be fooled into thinking of industrial steam in shunting-engine terms. In Europe, industrial railways were often very small affairs operated by diminutive 0-6-0 or even 0-4-0 tank locomotives. Train loads matched the size of the locomotives and lines very rarely exceeded a mile in length. Africa saw, during the1980s, some very impressive industrial railway operations - using ex-main line engines, often Garratts, over long and steeply graded routes.Train loads could exceed 1,000 tonnes and two-locomotive operation was often required, giving dramatic spectacles as they hauled their bulky commodities to the main line sidings. Even the gold mines, with their very large reserves of capital,

realised that steam power provided a sound investment as it moved vast tonnages of ore from which were extracted those few precious ounces of metal. With the availability of cheap second-hand engines still high it seems that many mines will continue using steam well into the 21st century as it provides a cheap and capital-efficient method of transportation.

The demise of steam has often had a strong effect on local communities, especially those of non-European descent. The water column, once closed, often meant the termination of a regular water supply, while the disappearance of the steam engine itself robbed some communities of their hot water. In areas where locomotives were coal-fired it meant a loss of fuel - either as a result of scavenging amongst ash piles for un-burned coal or where rough track caused spillage from the tender. Removal of steam power also has a rather more direct commercial impact, with the loss of many unskilled and semi-skilled jobs from the area and eventual decline and decay of complete towns - their

An enduring image of South African steam: Class 25NC 4-8-4 No. 3421 is seen hard at work leaving Ormonde, bound for Westminster, on the Bethlehem-Bloemfontein secondary main line, on June 23 1986. *John Laverick.*

sole reason for existence being the hungry fireboxes of steam locomotives. Towns like Horwich, Swindon and Shildon might have felt the effects of railway cutbacks - but to nothing like the same degree as in Africa.

The skill of the footplate crews must not be forgotten. During the decade they often had to contend with locomotives that were poorly maintained in view of a short life expectancy for steam. In addition, many African lines are notorious for their subtle changes of curvature and gradient which make operating a heavy steam-hauled train a very skilled job. Knowledge of the road is essential in all railway operations, but the need to think ahead is especially relevant with steam. Many crews also had to experience very long working hours. One duty may have been shared by two crews, each spending eight hours on the footplate and eight hours resting in the crew caboose coupled behind the engine. On long turns of duty, firemen often had to shovel nearly 20 tons of coal into the firebox during a return working, hence the need for a junior fireman on the footplate, whose main duty was to shift coal forward in the tender bunker. This was also a useful apprenticeship, for during his spell as 'coal pusher' he would learn the tricks of the footplate trade.

As a lasting memory of African steam I shall never forget a journey in the Eastern Cape riding from Maclear down the branch (which incidentally ran for nearly 200 miles!) - to Sterkstroom behind a '19D' class 4-8-2. We left just before dawn with a heavy frost on the ground, columns of white smoke and steam thrusting into the clear starry sky as we departed upgrade from

the terminus, steam leaking from between the coaches as the passengers enjoyed the benefit of the steam heating. About 15 minutes out we came to the first station, or more correctly, first siding. There were no lights, except for a small fire, and Africans were huddled around, waiting for the train. The driver spotted them and slowed. In the darkness they stumbled to the train. A green light from the guard, a whistle from the engine echoing around the hills and we were off again into the lightening dawn. Passing farmhouses and small communities we were providing a homely link to the outside world. The journey was to last all day - stopping at nearly every small station, taking water and cleaning fires every two hours, changing locomotives twice, and eventually reaching the main line about an hour after sunset - and an hour behind schedule.

During the journey we had discovered the colonial side of Africa with Glen Wallace providing a prefect reminder of Western Scotland – which was in complete contrast to the true African context of the branch, with distinctive station names such as Xuka Drift.

Below: The locomotive coaling stage at De Aaar motive power depot is filled from wagons which are propelled up this gantry - a gradient of about 1 in 15. On September 4 1983, Class 15A *Milly* is seen at work on the gantry, whilst in the foreground are stabled some of the shed's allocation of locomotives. *Peter Lockley.*

Above: A Class 25NC with the overnight passenger train from Bloemfontein to Bethlehem, in May 1985. *J.L.D. Price.*

Below: A pair of '15AR' class 4-8-2s, Nos. 2013 and 1784, are in charge of the 0800 Rosmead-Burgersdorp goods, on August 4 1982. *Duncan Cotterill.*

On June 18 1986, Class 25NC No. 3436 starts away from a wayside halt between Potfontein and Poupan, on the main line from De Aar to Kimberley. *John Laverick.*

Above: Clocolan yard in June 1985, as a Class 15F 4-8-2 shunts whilst running en route between Bloemfontein and Bethlehem. *Brian Dobbs.*

Right: South African steam in industry. A 1948-vintage 4-8-2, built by the North British Locomotive Company, is prepared for its next duty at Witbank Colliery, in June 1985. Industrial users in South Africa often bought new locomotives, of which this is an example. These were supplemented by former main line locomotives, purchased second-hand, made redundant by dieselisation or electrification. A far cry indeed from the four and six wheel tank engines which dominated the industrial scene in countries such as Great Britain (see page 61). *Brian Dobbs.*

Above: By 1989, Zimbabwe was the last remaining Garratt stronghold and this is a '16A' class 2-8-2+2-8-2, climbing hard on the Mulungwane Incline, with a freight train from Colleen Bawn to Bulawayo, on August 2 1986. The grade on is such that often locomotives have been known to stall and the only way to restart the train has been to reverse downhill and try again! *Hugh Ballantyne.*

Below: The 20th class Garratts were the largest steam locomotives at work on sub-standard gauges any where in the world during the 1980s. Equipped with mechanical stokers, they were the masters of any duty that required a hard 'slog' and in this view a 2,000-tons coal train is passing through the Hwange National Park, Zimbabwe, in July 1987, on its uphill struggle from Thomson Junction to Dete. *Lou Johnson.*

WORLD STEAM SINCE 1980

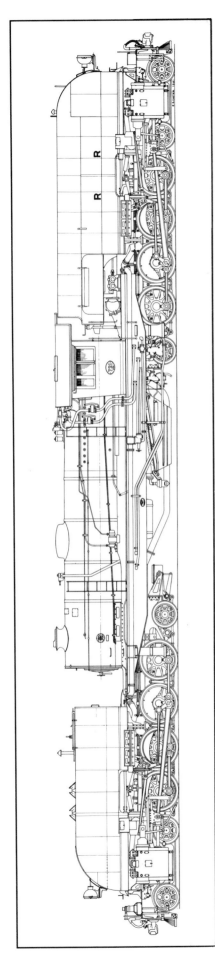

Above: This side-elevation of the NRZ 20A Class Garratt highlights the impressive nature of these powerful locomotives. In working order they weigh 225 tons and coal capacity is 14 tons. The leading and trailing tanks carry more than 7,500 gallons of water and the class was built by Beyer Peacock, of Manchester, UK, in 1954. *Drawn by Russell Carter.*

Left: No. 737, a 20th class Garratt, heads south towards Bulawayo with a coal train, from Thomson Junction, on August 7 1986. *Peter Lockley.*

Right: The overnight passenger train between Bulawayo and Victoria Falls remained in the hands of '15th' class Garratts for much of the decade. The desolate appearance of the platforms at Bulawayo at departure time (1900) belie the fact that this is one of Zimbabwe's few 'express' trains, still with 20 minutes to go to departure. *Lou Johnson.*

Below: The ZECO (Zimbabwe Engineering Company) railway workshops in Bulawayo have been responsible for the continued use of steam locomotives in Zimbabwe. On June 2 1988, a boiler from a Beyer Garratt is lifted for repair. The boiler proportions are especially clear in this view: the short, large diameter barrel and wide firebox being responsible for the superb steaming ability of these locomotives.
David C. Rodgers.

Below: Garratts galore! Bulawayo shed, in Zimbabwe, has an allocation in excess of 70 active locomotives, none of which are conventional types. Activity at the running shed is at its busiest during the late afternoon and here, recently-arrived engines are being watered and their fires cleaned in readiness for overnight stabling in the shed. The picture was taken in August 1987. *Lou Johnson.*

Left: Although noted for Garratt action, Zimbabwe did operate some conventional locomotives in the 1980s. For example, the colliery at Wankie was home to a number of 19th class 4-8-2s, some purchased new, whilst others were acquired second-hand from Rhodesian Railways. In July 1983, one of the 4-8-2s shunts in the colliery yards prior to taking loaded wagons to the main line connection at Thomson Junction. *J. L. D. Price.*

Above: A South African Railways GMA 4-8-2+2-8-4 Garratt, on loan to Zimbabwe, heads a heavy coal train away from Thomson Junction, in July 1983. These locomotives were used as a temporary measure whilst Zimbabwe's own fleet of Garratts was overhauled. Visitors must have sometimes wondered where all the country's own locomotives could be found, forshunting was also often in the hands of 14AR class 4-8-2s – also on loan from 'the South'. *Lou Johnson.*

WORLD STEAM SINCE 1980

CHAPTER 7:

THE AMERICAS

Above: The Brazilian line known as the Dona Teresa Cristina was the last railway in South America to use large engines hauling heavy trains. Here, Skoda 2-10-2 No. 208 (built in 1949) with more than 1,000 tons of coal on the tender drawbar, climbs towards Morrogrande, bound for the docks at Imbituba on October 23 1985. *John Hunt.*

The continent of America is vast and provides an incredible variety of climate, topography and railway. Historically, the railways of North America held a dominant role with the emphasis on super-power on heavy trains, a scene that many people wished was still with us today. Although connected by the Central American isthmus, the southern part of the continent produced a very different sort of railway, with development taking place in piecemeal fashion with no attempt to provide a unified network. In the Caribbean islands, Cuba has the largest network of lines.

Not surprisingly steam in the area has experienced very differing fortunes. The USA and Canada dispensed with steam almost completely during the 1950s, in their rapid quest for a modern rail transport system. Elsewhere in the region, steam has had a more lengthy life due mainly to lower traffic levels and the uncertain status of various national economies.

The 19th century witnessed a rapid growth in rail transport north of Panama, with a very large network reaching to virtually every viable corner of the USA and Canada. The same influences were also at work in Mexico, where a sizeable system was eventually built. Central and South America provided a very different picture with railways being constructed in a totally un-coordinated way using European and American capital. By the middle of the 20th century, the railway systems

Above: A diminutive 2-10-2 at work on the Argentinian coal-hauling Red Ferro Industrial Rio Turbio 2ft 6in gauge railway. Here RFIRT No. 113 waits at El Turbio in January 1987, before departure for Rio Gallegos, on the coast. This 255-kilometres line is the most southerly railway in the world. *Gunter Oczko.*

had reached their zenith with only Argentina and Chile boasting reasonably extensive systems.

For convenience, the whole of the Americas have been included in this chapter although as far as steam is concerned, the story belongs to South & Central America and Cuba. Most of the area south of the USA was either Spanish or Portuguese-speaking and there were close cultural and commercial links with Europe; railways were linked primarily with Great Britain. The USA also influenced many railways as a result of its geographical proximity. The overall result was to provide a unique mix of European and American railway technology, a blend of influences that could not be seen anywhere else in the world. Some railways were purely European in aspect whilst others were more akin to a slice of American railroading transported a few thousand miles south to a new home-land.

By the end of the 1970s, steam was in retreat, as American diesel salesmen, having completed their job at home and helped by favourable credit facilities, were successfully winning orders for new diesel motive power throughout the continent – especially where major national railway companies were concerned. The smaller railways were to prove less attractive to the salesmen and most retained their steam power well into the 1980s before succumbing to more modern methods.

South and Central America have a wide variety of

climates, from the tropical areas close to the equator to the cold, wet almost British-style weather of Southern Argentina and Chile. The most prominent topographical feature is the Andean mountain chain which stretches north-south along the western side of the continent. Although not as dramatic as the Andes, the plains of the Pampas of Argentina have had just as great an effect on the railways of the continent. The Americas have provided railway engineers with many challenges, especially where trans-Andean links have been built with many lines reaching altitudes in excess of ten thousand feet above sea level. Other records claimed by the continent include the world's most southerly steam-operated railway, the RFIRT from Rio Gallegos in Argentina.

The contrasts in steam operation offered to the enthusiast during the 1980s were varied and interesting. One of the greatest problems for visitors was the sheer size of the country, with large distances to be covered between centres of working steam. Those who made the effort were well rewarded, for the offerings that each railway made were often

On the Esquel branch in Argentina, No. 109, a Henschel-built 2-8-2, takes water at Nahuel Pan, with a mixed train, in November 1988. In 1989, this branch was still steam-worked. *Gunter Oczko.*

Above: The massive proportions of these 2-10-4s are clearly illustrated here; looking at this view, it is difficult to believe that that the Dona Teresa Cristina line is laid only to metre gauge! *Phil Girdlestone.*

Right: The roundhouse at Sao Joao del Rei was partially destroyed by fire, but despite having no roof, it remained in use until the line closed to normal service in the early 1980s. Here No. 38, a Baldwin-built 4-6-0, prepares for its next duty. *Tony Eaton.*

unique, either in motive power or in character. South America was a continent which offered quality, rather than quantity of steam operation.

Brazil was home to two railways of special note. The 2ft 6in gauge VFCO, from Sao Joao del Rei, operated two lines from its delightful terminus. The railway had survived in an area where road transport was unable to compete, and provided the local population with a vital link to the outside world. As road transport was gradually improved the need for the railway diminished and by the middle of the decade it had closed to normal revenue-earning service. However, surprisingly for Brazil, local interest in the railway was such that a tourist-style operation was commenced which meant survival for at least part of the superb fleet of American built oil-fired locomotives, including 2-8-0s, 4-6-0s and a brace of really special 4-4-0s, all based at the half derelict roundhouse which had suffered fire damage and was never rebuilt. Rolling stock was also purely American in style, with wooden-bodied coaches sporting end balconies, which made for a pleasant ride through the often spectacular countryside.

The other major line in Brazil was the Dona Cristina Teresa coal-hauling line, built to metre gauge and based from Tubarao in the southern coastal area of the country. The line itself survived on hauling coal from the mines to the power station, with surplus output running through to the port at Imbituba. Although only metre gauge, the line epitomised all that was so impressive about American-style railroading, with large locomotives and heavy trains. From some photographs, it is hard to distinguish that the railway is narrow gauge, for all components of the scene are in proportion and the railway could well be standard gauge. In reality the line and its locomotives were a three-quarter size interpretation of the typical coal hauling 'road' in the USA. The line was also unique in that it was the last to operate 2-10-4s, a wheel arrangement known as 'Texan'. With their four-wheel trailing bogies the engines were able to be built with large fireboxes, making them excellent providers of steam, even with heavy trains.

Above: Until 1983, a 2ft 6in gauge system ran both east and west from the little Brazilian town of Sao Joao del Rei, for a nearly 200 kilometres. Motive power, all supplied by Baldwin of the USA, included 4-6-0s, 2-8-0s and two 4-4-0s. In this scene, No.21, one of the 4-4-0s, crosses the Rio das Mortes near Aureliano Mourao with the thrice-weekly 'mixed' on July 1 1982. *Nick Tindall.*

The Guayaquil & Quito line, in Ecuador, has suffered its fair share of landslides and washouts. In mid-1988, the daily 'mixed' to from Guayaquil was terminating at the little wayside station of Alausi, where the engine stayed in the street overnight before returning to base the following day. Baldwin-built 2-8-0 No.45 is captured waiting patiently for departure the following day, in August 1988. *Nick Tindall.*

Left: The American influence in motive power and rolling stock is clearly shown here as G&Q No.44, another Baldwin 'Consolidation' wheels a sizeable mixed train through the town of Milagro, in Equador, on August 16 1988
Paul Stratford.

Paraguay offered the enthusiast the only 100% steam-operated national railway in the continent, in the 1980s. The line from the capital of Asuncion to the Argentinian border at Encarnacion provided a nominal train service to the population with equipment dating from the opening of the line, in 1912. Paraguay is not noted for its national economic strength, and this is reflected in the degree of investment on the railways. They have seen virtually nothing in the way of new equipment since opening and although various feasibility studies have been made in respect of modernisation, lack of

finance has meant that these good intentions are unlikely to come to fruition.

The largest concentration of railways was to be found in Argentina, where British investment fostered the construction of a large network especially in the flatter Pampas. Initially construction was commenced by a number of individual companies each having little regard for the interests of the others. This lack of co-operation eventually resulted in Argentina having three major gauges: broad, standard and metre gauges - with a limited mileage of pure narrow gauge. As far as

steam was concerned, it was the latter that provided the interest during the 1980s, with the Esquel branch in the lee of the Andes and the RFIRT at Rio Gallegos both operating wholly steam-hauled services.

Elsewhere on the continent, operational steam was to be found in small quantities on a number of lines. Ecuador and Peru probably offered the most, with the Guayaquil and Quito line as the most dramatic. It provided the visitor with a microcosm of South American rail-roading with virtually every item of equipment originating from the USA. The line itself provided enormous variety in scenery, from the flatter areas around the terminus at Guayaquil, through streets in towns and villages to the dramatic and famous climb at the Devil's Nose.

The great surprise of the 1980s was the granting of permission to railway enthusiast groups for visits to railway installations in Cuba. It was known that steam did exist on the island but in what quantities was totally unpredictable. Due to large diesel orders being given coverage in the railway press it was guessed, quite

correctly, that the main line system would be devoid of steam. Where the interest was bound to lie would be in the numerous sugar mills that dotted the landscape right across the island. Prior to the Revolution of 1956, a few American enthusiasts had made brief forays into the cane-fields and had reported a remarkable collection of locomotives of various gauges.

In the first few years of the decade, a number of visits were made to the island and soon it became evident that Cuba held a superb collection of steam railways. Most sugar mills on the island had a fleet of between five and ten locomotives and based on this average it

WORLD STEAM SINCE 1980

appeared that there would be a total of some five hundred engines. What made life interesting was that very few of the locomotives were common in design and there was a wide variety of gauges, including some not to be seen elsewhere in the world. After some 20 or so mills had been visited, a few other facts came to light. Firstly, each mill often had a small engine for pilot duties around the mill site and usually this was the oldest locomotive available. Secondly, the larger engines, used primarily for cane haulage from the fields, were regularly to be seen traversing the main line system as they travelled considerable distances from the mills in their quest to collect the harvest. Thirdly, we found that many mills operated a rudimentary passenger service for the benefit of their workforces, and although most of these services were in the hands of small diesel railcars there were occasional steam worked services. Finally, Cuba has a significant number of fireless locomotives which are charged with steam from the processing plants. To many people, these are not considered to be 'real' engines at all and are ignored; however, in an age where careful use of power resources is encouraged they do provide a useful method of short distance transportation using what would otherwise be wasted energy.

All the mills in Cuba are referred to as 'Centrals' and,

in keeping with the high political profile of the country, many are named after famous freedom fighters from such notable persons as Abraham Lincoln to rather less known Cuban independence fighters - Guillermo Moncada being an example. Other mills are named after countries where an independence struggle is under way - Central Guatemala - whilst others have a rather more intriguing title such as Central Australia which could either be stating a simple geographical fact – or it might suggest that this country is about to suffer a violent communist uprising !

Casting my mind back to my first visit in May 1980, I remember that the atmosphere was quite tense. Sugar is an important part of the Cuban economy and as such was treated with almost military importance. Visits were strictly conducted and often it was impossible to enter into the sugar mill itself; our activities were limited to the yards and rail facilities. At one mill, I remember that even when we were standing outside an engine shed which was clearly full of steam locomotives, the mill staff were still very reluctant to admit that they

Below: On October 7 1985, Baldwin-built 3ft 6in gauge 2-8-0 No. 17 (built in 1935) stands at Sibambe, Ecquador, awaiting its next turn of duty. *John Hunt.*

Above: In Uruguay, a handsome 'N' class 2-6-0 pauses during a spell of pleasant late afternoon sun at Quegay, near Paysandu, in November 1988.
J. L. D. Price.

Right: Tank engines were few and far between in South America, except where used on suburban services. A common ploy to extend their range, was to add a redundant tender from a scrapped locomotive, as seen here at Encarnacion shed, on June 11 1985. *Ron White/ Colourail.*

possessed such items! What was found was beyond belief, with many interesting locomotives seen by enthusiasts for the first time in 20 years ! My favourite recollection is a visit to Central Ruben Martinez Villena, where the railway foreman said: "We have a locomotive over a hundred years old." At the back of the shed we found a small 0-4-2 tank engine which was built in 1874 - just 106 years old! The sugar industry is seasonal, with a great deal of activity concentrated into five or six months during the harvest. The remainder of the year is available for uninterrupted maintenance and so engines with a nominal age of 50 years have in fact probably only worked for about 22 years, and during that period have been well well cared for.

Looking ahead to the last decade of the 20th century, the life of steam must surely come to an end on the South American continent, with the probable exception of Cuba. Most railways have at least expressed an intention to dieselise and whilst this commitment remains the future cannot be too hopeful. Those who have not expressed any intentions for modernisation must surely be likely candidates for closure, such is the competitive nature of the today's transport marketplace. Cuba will probably be the 'odd man out' and steam is likely to stay in use for the foreseeable future, with a slow decline in actual operating numbers inevitable as engines inevitably become irreparable due to old age and fatigue.

The Paraguayan State Railway must rank as the railway suffering from the lowest level of investment worldwide. Most of its standard gauge equipment dates from 1910, when the railway was opened. In this view, 2-6-0 No. 60, built by the North British Locomotive Company in 1910, stands at the head of train No.2 in General Artigas station. *Chris West.*

Above: Typical of the general condition of the Paraguayan railway generally, are the grass covered tracks on the main line! In this view, the cool, crisp air helps the photographer to capture the atmosphere of this fascinating railway as North British Locomotive Company 2-6-0 No. 103 (built 1910) passes with one of the weekly trains from Encarnacion to Ascuncion, in November 1983. Worthy of note is that railway is named the FC Presidente Carlos Antonio Lopez. *John Hunt.*

Right: Guaqui, on the southern shore of Lake Titicaca, in Bolivia, on October 16 1985. Baldwin 2-10-2 No. 704 is shunting on the dockside as the *Ollanta* (built by Earles of Hull, in 1930) prepares for its next sailing; the lake provides a vital link between railheads of the area. The steam crane was also British built – by Smith & Rodley, of Leeds, Yorkshire. *John Hunt.*

On the Hunacayo-Huancavelica line, in Peru, Hunslet-built 2-8-0 No. 107 pauses to take on water in mountainous surroundings on Friday October 10 1985. *Gavin Morrison.*

Facing page, top: Tank engines were not common in South America, where their limited water capacity was not well-suited to the long distances between towns. Here, metre gauge Hunslet 2-8-4T No. 553 (built in 1912) shunts at Oruro in the Bolivian foothills of the Andes. *John Hunt.*

Facing page, lower: The mountainous areas of South America provided railway engineers with a major challenge. The FCCSA, in Peru, had to contend with many natural obstacles and on October 14 1985 a passenger train hauled by Baldwin 2-8-2 No. 123 and Henschel 2-8-2 No. 122 is seen climbing between Izcuchaca and El Arco. The train is dwarfed by the awe-inspiring backdrop of mountains. *John Hunt.*

Above: The line from Huancayo to Huancavelica in Peru boasted superb scenery, heavy grades and high altitudes. Here, a typical consist heads uphill near Larmenta, between Huancayo and Mariscal Caceres, on October 11 1985, in the charge of Hunslet 2-8-0 No. 107, built in 1936. *John Hunt.*

Left: 2-8-0 No. 107 again, seen this time in the valley of the Mantara river (a tributary of the Amazon) working a train from Huancavelica to Huancayo, on October 29 1983. This picture was taken between Mariscal Caceres and Izcuchaca. *John Hunt.*

Right: No. 106, a Baldwin-built 2-8-2 of 1927 vintage, leaves Pilchaca, Peru, with a train from Huancayo to Huancavelica, amidst spectacular and rocky scenery. *John Hunt.*

Below: Working hard at Paupoy, between Cusco and Huaracondo, Peru, are 2-8-2s Nos. 123 and 122, with a passenger train, on October 14 1985. *John Hunt.*

At the Boris Luis Santa Coloma Mill, Cuba, an Alco-built 2-6-0 struggles with a heavy load of cane-cars on the final approach to the mill yards. March 11 1988. *Nick Tindall.*

Above: Orlando Nodarse Mill had only a small track mileage; its working engine in March 1981 was No.1211, a beautiful narrow gauge Baldwin engine. *Lou Johnson.*

Right: Orenstein & Koppel of Germany built this pleasant 0-4-0 fireless locomotive in 1912. Often ignored by enthusiasts as not being 'real' steam engines, this particular locomotive is seen working at Ciro Redondo Mill, in Cuba, during the 1981 sugar season. *Lou Johnson.*

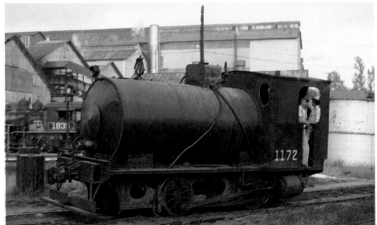

Below: This 0-4-2T, seen here in 1981, is dwarfed by the modern freight cars it is shunting. Built in 1878 by Baldwin, it first saw use in mainland America before being sold to a Cuban sugar-mill. It is only rarely that 'new' locomotives are discovered of this age and in 1980 it was a sensation to discover this engine tucked at the back of its depot at the Ruben Martinez Villena Mill. *Lou Johnson*

CONCLUSION

Above: To accompany this conclusion, I have chosen a series of pictures at random, showing a variety of countries and highlighting unusual, impressive or simply bizarre aspects of steam operation worldwide in the 1980s. This beautiful view, entitled 'Raj Reflection' by the photographer, depicts India's Eastern Railway, between Krishnanagar and Shantipur, as a 2-4-0T passes at sunset, during 1981. *John Hunt.*

The 1980s started with a very poor outlook for the future of steam in main line service. It appeared to be the end of an innovative form of transportation that was about to be replaced completely by more modern forms of motive power. By the end of the decade, many countries were still using limited amounts of steam motive power and all had not been doom and gloom, as predicted ten years earlier.

With hindsight, many countries realised that modern technology, although offering many advantages in theory, had limitations in practice especially where facilities and labour were not in line with the often critical technical requirements of the modern methods of power. It would have been more responsible for them to have modernised at a slower and more considered rate, so that technical innovation was matched with improvements in maintenance facilities, increased education of the workforce and, most

importantly, an increase in available finances for spares and capital investment.

This lesson was unfortunately learned too late for any noticeable impact on operational steam power. Had this fact been appreciated in the 1960s, then this book would have been able to tell a different story and far greater numbers of active steam locomotives would have been available for service. Modern traction would have been restricted to the more developed nations, with a subsequent saving of capital resources by the poorer countries for other important projects.

Facing page: A stirring scene in Pakistan, on the steeply-graded branch between Khewra and Dandot, on January 7 1988, as British-built 'SGS' 0-6-0 No. 2470 storms through the arid, rocky terrain. *John Laverick.*

Left: It's November 1987 at Krishnarajanagar with 'YG' class 2-8-2 No. 4344 and its crew awaiting departure with a Mysore-Arsikere passenger train.

During my travels I have learned that railway staff have been generally enthusiastic about steam. They were familiar with its ways and were able to cope easily with demands and needs. It employed technology that could be experienced, seen and learned at first hand, whereas with diesel and electric power there are many systems which required a perfect scientific under-

Above: Although it is easy to capture the purely pictorial elements of a scene, it is much more difficult to convey the noise, smells and general hustle and bustle of an Indian railway station. This excellent picture shows the characteristic chaos associated with train departures in this part of the world! No. 639, a 'BS' class locomotive, is in charge of a train from Ranchi to Lohardaga, in Central India, during December 1984. *Peter Barlow.*

Right: A well-filled train in Nepal! On November 28 1984, 0-6-0-2T *Surjya* leaves Janakpurdham for Jaynagar, with passengers seemingly clinging to every last hand and foothold on the locomotive and train. Roof-riding is an everyday fact of life in the Indian sub-continent! *Hugh Ballantyne.*

Above: 'WP' class 'Pacific' No. 7156 makes a leisurely departure (in true Indian style!) from Lucknow, in November 1984. Although outwardly very robust-looking, every Indian driver arrived on duty with a box full of 'bits and pieces' required to keep the locomotive running through the shift! The box contained such essential items as fencing wire, large hammers and silver paint - for no matter what the mechanical condition was, it was important that the engine *looked* well-kept! *Peter Barlow.*

standing. For example, a micro-processor gives no visual clues as to what happens inside - it is harder for people to conceive its purpose. This is in complete contrast to the old-fashioned steam locomotive, which has a very visual and easily understood mechanical simplicity, and it is much more tolerant of indifferent treatment and maintenance than sensitive diesel locomotives. The last decade of the 20th century will probably see the total eclipse of steam, with a few small exceptions. By the year 2000, the necessary adjustments to education should have been implemented and with greater understanding electric and

Above: In January 1987, 'WP' class 4-6-2 No. 7350 is at the head of a Puri-Khurda Road local train at Jankideipur, on the South Eastern Railway. By the end of the 1980s, the 'WPs' had been relegated to less-important duties such as this. *Gunter Oczko.*

Left: In January 1981, 'CWD' class 2-8-2 No. 5606 leaves Rawalpinid, in Pakistan, with a train for Attock city. *John Hunt.*

117

Facing page: The Hawaiian Philippine sugar mill, on the island of Negros, hosted an immaculate fleet of bagasse-fired locomotives. An unusual feature is the registration plate, carried beneath the lamp on this Baldwin 0-6-0, presumably entitling the locomotive to use the public highway! *Tony Eaton.*

Left: Only a few kilometres separate the sun-kissed beaches and poolside bars of Varadero, from this charming Cuban backwoods operation. A Vulcan Ironworks 2-8-0, built in 1916, heads a lengthy train back to the mill at Humberto, Alvarez, in March 1988. *Nick Tindall.*

Below: A last look at the Devil's Nose, in Ecquador. Baldwin 2-8-0 No. 17 is seen approaching Zig Zag Bajo, on the climb to Zig Zag Alto, on October 7 1985. *John Hunt.*

diesel traction will become more effective especially in Third World countries. So, with regret I close with a farewell to steam. It has provided the world with a trusted form of transport for more than 150 years. It has been responsible for opening up vast areas of the world to civilisation and has provided millions of inhabitants in all parts of the globe with jobs, links to friends and relatives, trade and commerce. It was a job well done.

The Second World War did much to lengthen the life of steam. It provided a period of devastation which railways took years to overcome. This American-built 'S160' class 2-8-0 was delivered in an attempt to accelerate recovery, and is seen here, more than 30 years later, heading away from the mountains at Kardesgedici, Turkey. *Jim Livesey.*

South African steam ran throughout the 1980s, and into the 1990s. Here, Class 25NC 4-8-4 No. 3474 leaves Vryhof for Mafikeng, on June 15 1986. *John Laverick.*